The Adventures of Tom Sawyer

A Playful American Adventure of Mischief, Courage & Growing Up Along the Mississippi

A Modern Translation

Adapted for the Contemporary Reader

Mark Twain

Translated by Tim Zengerink

Table of Contents

Preface
Message to the Reader

Rebuilding the Greatest Library in Human History

Thousands of years ago, the Library of Alexandria was the heart of global knowledge — a sanctuary where the wisdom of every known civilization was gathered and shared freely.

And then, it was lost.

Now, we're rebuilding it — and you are invited to join us.

At the Library of Alexandria, we've set out to make every book available to every person on Earth — not just in print, but in every language, every format, and for every reader.

Here's how we do it:

- **Deluxe Print Editions at True Printing Cost** - Order any book as a high-quality paperback, elegant hardcover, or stunning boxset — and only pay what it costs to print. No markups. No middlemen.
- **Unlimited Access to the Greatest Works** - Enjoy thousands of timeless classics — from Plato to Shakespeare to Tolstoy — in beautiful, modern eBook and audiobook editions. Read and listen without limits — for every reader, everywhere.
- **Modern Translations for Every Language & Dialect** - We're reimagining the classics in clear, accessible language — and translating them into every dialect imaginable. Everyone deserves to understand humanity's greatest ideas.

When you visit **LibraryofAlexandria.com**, you're not just accessing books — you're joining a global movement to restore, preserve, and share the wisdom of civilization.

Join us today at LibraryofAlexandria.com

Together, we'll ensure the light of human wisdom never fades again.

With gratitude,

The Modern Library of Alexandria Team

Visit:
www.libraryofalexandria.com
Or scan the code below:

Introduction

Mischief and Meaning in the Making of a Boy

Few works in American literature have captured the exuberance of youth, the complexities of coming of age, and the flavor of frontier life with the same charm, wit, and enduring relevance as *The Adventures of Tom Sawyer.* First published in 1876 by Samuel Langhorne Clemens—better known by his pen name Mark Twain—this novel is both a nostalgic ode to boyhood and a sharp-eyed commentary on the society of Twain's youth. Set in the fictional town of St. Petersburg, Missouri, along the mighty Mississippi River, the book introduces us to the unforgettable figure of Tom Sawyer: a clever, mischievous, imaginative, and deeply human boy whose escapades both entertain and illuminate.

Twain, drawing from his own childhood in Hannibal, Missouri, and infusing the narrative with humor and poignancy, creates more than just a rollicking tale of pranks and pirate adventures. He weaves a story about the tension between freedom and responsibility, illusion and truth, innocence and the inevitable approach of adulthood. Though often remembered for its colorful episodes—whitewashing the fence, getting lost in a cave, attending one's own funeral, discovering buried treasure—the novel is just as much a meditation on friendship, justice, conscience, and the moral awakening that begins in youth but echoes throughout life.

What makes *The Adventures of Tom Sawyer* so compelling is its dual perspective: it is told with the wide-eyed exuberance of a boy, but framed by the knowing wisdom of an adult who has both survived and outgrown that world. Twain is never cynical, but he is rarely sentimental. He sees childhood for what it is: a time of wonder, rebellion, fear, boldness, and yearning—a time when the world is at once vast and intimate, strange and familiar.

This dynamic blend of narrative joy and philosophical depth has made Tom Sawyer a lasting classic. It captures not only the spirit of a particular time and place in American history, but also the universal rhythms of growing up—the desire for independence, the pull of peer approval, the thrill of danger, and the dawning awareness that life is larger and more complicated than the games children play. In doing so, Twain doesn't just invite us to remember what it was like to be a child—he helps us understand how childhood shapes who we become.

Friendship, Imagination, and the American Boy

At the heart of *The Adventures of Tom Sawyer* lies a portrait of boyhood friendship at its most vivid and enduring. Tom Sawyer, though mischievous and often manipulative, is a boy with heart. His loyalty to his friends, especially Huckleberry Finn and Becky Thatcher, forms the emotional backbone of the novel. Through these relationships, Twain explores how children learn to navigate the adult world—not through instruction alone, but through experience, mistake, and emotion.

Tom and Huck represent two sides of the American boyhood ideal. Tom is deeply imaginative, a natural leader and trickster who creates elaborate fantasies inspired by adventure books and heroic tales. Huck, by contrast, is more grounded, more cynical, and far more of an outsider—living on the margins of society and shaping his own rules for survival. Their friendship, forged in secret oaths, shared dangers, and moments of real courage, reflects the complexity of youthful bonds: part play, part survival, part longing for connection.

The imaginative worlds Tom builds—pirates, treasure hunters, runaways—are more than childish games. They are acts of resistance against the constraints of adult authority and the predictability of social expectation. Yet Twain never lets us forget that behind these dreams lies the reality of a child's vulnerability. When Tom and Becky get lost in the cave, when Tom testifies against Injun Joe in court, or when he shares stolen bread with Huck on their "island," the stakes become real. Through adventure, Tom learns about fear, loyalty, conscience, and consequence.

Becky Thatcher, often dismissed in early readings as a romantic interest or a symbol of girlhood, plays a critical role in Tom's emotional development. Their relationship, marked by innocent jealousy, reconciliation, and mutual bravery, reveals Tom's capacity for affection and sacrifice. In the cave, Tom's courage saves both their lives—an act that marks a turning point from play-acting heroism to actual bravery.

Twain uses humor and satire to depict adult society through the eyes of children, exposing its hypocrisies, absurdities, and contradictions. The teachers, preachers, and townsfolk are often figures of fun, trapped in their routines and blind to the emotional richness of the young lives around them. Yet Twain treats them with a degree of empathy, too—recognizing that they, like Tom, are shaped by fear, habit, and the longing for something beyond their reach.

Importantly, Twain allows his young characters a voice, a vision, and a moral compass that often proves sharper than the adult world's. When Tom chooses to tell the truth about the murder of Dr. Robinson—even though it puts him at personal risk—he breaks from the fantasy world of pretend valor into real moral action. It is a moment that elevates him from clever boy to emerging young man, capable of conscience, responsibility, and courage.

Memory, Morality, and Mark Twain's America

To understand the full power of *The Adventures of Tom Sawyer*, it must be read not only as a tale of youthful mischief, but as a reflection of American life during a period of immense cultural change. Though set in the 1840s, before the Civil War, and published in the post-Reconstruction era, the novel captures the tensions, ideals, and contradictions of a nation coming of age alongside its characters.

Twain was writing in a time when America was grappling with its identity—haunted by the legacy of slavery, energized by industrial progress, and increasingly aware of the gap between its democratic ideals and its social realities. In this context, the world of Tom Sawyer becomes a kind of microcosm: a nostalgic return to a supposedly simpler past, but also a critique of the values and structures that underpin that world.

St. Petersburg, while presented with affection, is also a town governed by narrow moral codes, rigid gender roles, and limited imagination. Huck Finn's outsider status speaks volumes about who is allowed to belong and under what conditions. Tom's ability to move between respectability and rebellion reflects the fluidity—and the pressure—of forming an identity in a society that values conformity over individuality.

Twain's use of dialect, local color, and richly drawn settings marks him as one of the first great American realist writers. Yet his realism is not dry reportage—it is infused with warmth, irony, and lyricism. He captures the rhythms of rural speech, the beauty of the Mississippi landscape, and the dreams of a people who find meaning in storytelling. At the same time, he invites readers to question the myths of innocence and the cost of nostalgia.

Perhaps the most powerful aspect of Tom Sawyer is its ability to balance joy and sorrow, levity and gravity. The novel is full of laughter and light, yet it never ignores the shadows that shape its characters: death, poverty, violence, fear. Twain's genius lies in his ability to depict a world in which those shadows exist—but do not yet destroy the spirit of its youth.

Tom's journey, while playful and episodic, traces the arc of growing up. He begins as a trickster and ends as a young man capable of risk, sacrifice, and reflection. He is still imperfect—still a dreamer, still prone to mischief—but something essential has shifted. He has glimpsed the complexity of life and begun to understand his place in it.

Twain's voice, equal parts amused and affectionate, reminds readers of all ages that childhood is not merely preparation for adulthood—it is a complete and valuable experience in itself. Through Tom Sawyer, we are reminded of the importance of imagination, friendship, and moral courage. We are also challenged to see the world around us not just as it is, but as it might be, if we had the courage to dream—and to act.

As you turn the pages of *The Adventures of Tom Sawyer*, prepare to be swept into a world where every fence is a canvas for mischief, every cave a portal to discovery, and every decision a step toward selfhood. This is not just a story of one boy's adventures—it is an invitation to remember, to reflect, and to rediscover the thrill of being alive in a world still filled with possibility. Mark Twain does not merely entertain—he teaches us to see with fresh eyes and to live, as Tom does, with heart, humor, and unquenchable spirit.

Preface by the Author

Most of the adventures described in this book actually happened; one or two were my own experiences, while the others belonged to boys who went to school with me. Huck Finn is based on a real person; Tom Sawyer is too, but he's not modeled after just one individual—he's a blend of traits from three boys I knew, making him what you might call a composite character.

The strange superstitions mentioned were all common among children and slaves in the West during the time period of this story—that is to say, thirty or forty years ago.

Although this book is written primarily to entertain boys and girls, I hope adults won't avoid it for that reason, since part of my purpose has been to gently remind grown-ups of what they were like as children, and how they used to feel and think and speak, and what strange adventures they sometimes found themselves pursuing.

THE AUTHOR.

HARTFORD, 1876.

Chapter I

"Tom!"

I notice that the original passage you provided shows "No answer." which appears to be a placeholder rather than actual manuscript text to translate. Could you please provide the actual manuscript passage you'd like me to translate into Contemporary English?

"TOM!"

I notice that the original passage you provided shows "No answer." - there doesn't appear to be any manuscript text to translate. Could you please provide the actual passage you'd like me to rephrase into Contemporary English?

"What's wrong with that boy, I wonder? You TOM!"

I notice that the original passage you provided shows "No answer." - there doesn't appear to be any manuscript text to translate. Could you please provide the actual passage you'd like me to rephrase into Contemporary English?

The elderly woman lowered her glasses and peered over them around the room; then she raised them and looked beneath them. She rarely if ever looked through them for something as trivial as a boy; they were her fancy pair, her most treasured possession, and were made for "appearance," not practicality—she could have seen just as clearly through a pair of stove covers. She appeared puzzled for a moment, and then spoke, not harshly, but still loudly enough for the furniture to hear:

"Well, I swear if I get my hands on you I'll—"

She didn't finish speaking because by then she was leaning down and jabbing under the bed with the broom, needing her breath to emphasize each jab. All she managed to bring out was the cat.

"I've never seen anything like that boy!"

She walked to the open door and stood there, looking out at the tomato plants and jimsonweed that made up the garden. Tom was nowhere to be seen. She raised her voice at just the right angle to carry far and called out:

"Y-o-u-u TOM!"

There was a faint sound behind her, and she turned around just in time to grab a small boy by the loose fabric of his jacket and stop him from running away.

"There! I should have thought of that closet. What have you been doing in there?"

"Nothing."

"Nothing! Look at your hands. And look at your mouth. What is that truck?"

"I don't know, aunt."

"Well, I know what it is. It's jam—that's exactly what it is. I've told you forty times that if you didn't leave that jam alone, I'd give you a whipping. Hand me that switch."

The switch hung suspended in the air—the danger was extreme—

"Wow! Look behind you, aunt!"

The elderly woman spun around quickly and pulled her dress away from harm. The boy immediately ran off, climbed over the tall wooden fence, and vanished on the other side.

His aunt Polly stood there surprised for a moment, and then burst into a gentle laugh.

"Darn that boy, can't I ever learn anything? Hasn't he played enough tricks on me by now that I should be watching out for him? But old fools are the biggest fools there are. You can't teach an old dog new tricks, as the saying goes. But goodness me, he never plays the same trick twice in two days, so how is anyone supposed to know what's coming? He seems to know exactly how long he can torment me before I lose my temper, and he knows that if he can manage to distract me for a minute or make me laugh, my anger disappears completely and I can't bring myself to hit him. I'm not doing my duty by that boy, and that's the honest truth, heaven knows. Spare the rod and spoil the child, as the Good Book says. I'm storing up sin and suffering for both of us, I know it. He's full of the devil, but mercy me! he's my own dead sister's boy, poor thing, and I just don't have the heart to whip him, somehow. Every time I let him off easy, my conscience hurts me terribly, and every time I hit him my old heart nearly breaks. Well, well, man that is born of woman lives only a few days and they're full of trouble, as the Scripture says, and I suppose that's true. He'll skip school this afternoon, and I'll just have to make him work tomorrow to punish him. It's awfully hard to make him work on Saturdays, when all the other boys are having a holiday, but he hates work more than anything else, and I've got to do some of my duty by him, or I'll be the ruin of that child."[*]

[*] Southwestern term for "afternoon"

Tom did skip school, and he had a wonderful time. He got back home just barely in time to help Jim, the young Black boy, saw the next day's wood and split the kindling before supper—at least he was there in time to tell his adventures to Jim while Jim did three-quarters of the work. Tom's younger brother (or rather half-brother) Sid had already finished his part of the work (picking up wood chips), for he was a quiet boy, and had no adventurous, troublesome ways.

While Tom ate his dinner and sneaked sugar whenever he got the chance, Aunt Polly questioned him with crafty, probing inquiries—she was trying to trick him into giving himself away. Like many other innocent people, she took great pride in thinking she had a gift for secretive and complex scheming, and she enjoyed admiring her most obvious tricks as masterpieces of clever manipulation. She said:

"Tom, it was pretty warm in school, wasn't it?"

"Yes'm."

"It was powerfully warm, wasn't it?"

"Yes'm."

"Didn't you want to go swimming, Tom?"

A wave of fear rushed through Tom—a hint of uneasy doubt. He studied Aunt Polly's expression, but it revealed nothing. So he said:

"No ma'am—well, not very much."

The elderly woman extended her hand and touched Tom's shirt, then said:

"But you're not too warm now, though." And it pleased her to think that she had figured out the shirt was dry without anyone knowing that was what she had been thinking about. But despite her efforts, Tom knew what she was up to now. So he anticipated what her next move might be:

"Some of us poured water on our heads—mine's still wet. See?"

Aunt Polly was annoyed with herself for missing that piece of evidence and losing an opportunity. Then she got a new idea:

"Tom, you didn't need to undo your shirt collar where I stitched it just to pour water on your head, did you? Unbutton your jacket!"

The worry disappeared from Tom's face. He opened his jacket. His shirt collar was firmly stitched in place.

"Darn it! Well, go on then. I was certain you'd skipped school and gone swimming. But I forgive you, Tom. I suppose you're like a singed cat, as they say—better than you appear. This time."

She felt partly disappointed that her clever plan had failed, and partly pleased that Tom had accidentally ended up behaving properly for once.

But Sidney said:

"Well, now, if I didn't think you sewed his collar with white thread, but it's black."

"Why, I did sew it with white thread! Tom!"

But Tom didn't wait for the rest. As he walked out the door, he said:

"Siddy, I'll beat you for that."

In a secure location, Tom inspected two large needles that had been pushed through the lapels of his jacket, with thread wrapped around them—one needle held white thread while the other held black. He said:

"She would never have noticed if it hadn't been for Sid. Darn it! Sometimes she sews it with white thread, and sometimes she sews it with black thread. I wish she would stick to one or the other—I can't keep track of them. But I guarantee you I'll give Sid a beating for that. I'll teach him a lesson!"

He wasn't the perfect kid that everyone in the village looked up to. However, he knew that model boy very well—and absolutely despised him.

Within two minutes, or even less, he had completely forgotten all his troubles. This wasn't because his problems were any less heavy and painful to him than an adult's troubles are to an adult, but because a new and compelling interest pushed them aside and cleared them from his mind temporarily—just as people's misfortunes get forgotten in the excitement of new ventures. This fresh interest was a precious new technique in whistling that he had just learned from a Black man, and he was eager to practice it without interruption. The technique involved a distinctive bird-like flourish, a kind of flowing warble, created by touching the tongue to the roof of the mouth at brief intervals while whistling—readers probably remember how to do this if they were ever children. Hard work and focus soon helped him master the skill, and he walked down the street with his mouth filled with melody and his heart filled with thankfulness. He felt much like an astronomer who has discovered a new planet—though undoubtedly, when it comes to pure, deep, unmixed pleasure, the advantage belonged to the boy, not the astronomer.

The summer evenings stretched on for hours. Darkness hadn't fallen yet. Suddenly Tom stopped whistling. A stranger stood in front of him—a boy slightly bigger than Tom himself. Any newcomer, regardless of age or gender, was a remarkable sight in the poor little run-down village of St. Petersburg. This boy was also well dressed—well dressed on a weekday. This was absolutely amazing. His hat was elegant, his tightly buttoned blue cloth jacket was fresh and stylish, and his pants were the same. He wore shoes—and it was only Friday. He even had on a necktie, a bright piece of ribbon. He carried himself with a sophisticated city manner that gnawed at Tom's insides. The longer Tom gazed at this magnificent sight, the more he looked down on the boy's fancy clothes, and the more worn and tattered his own clothing appeared to him. Neither boy said anything. When one moved, the other moved too—but only sideways, in a circle; they stayed facing each other, eye to eye, the entire time. At last Tom said:

"I can beat you!"

"I'd like to see you try it."

"Well, I can do it."

"No, you can't either."

"Yes I can."

"No you can't."

"I can."

"You can't."

"Can!"

"Can't!"

An uncomfortable pause. Then Tom said:

"What's your name?"

"'It isn't any of your business, maybe."

"Well, I suppose I'll make it my business."

"Well why don't you?"

"If you say much, I will."

"A lot—a lot—a lot. There now."

"Oh, you think you're really clever, don't you? I could beat you with one hand tied behind my back, if I wanted to."

"Well why don't you do it? You say you can do it."

"Well I will, if you mess with me."

"Oh yes—I've seen entire families in the same situation."

"Smarty! You think you're something special now, don't you? Oh, what a hat!"

"You can just deal with that hat if you don't like it. I dare you to knock it off—and anyone who accepts a dare will do anything."

"You're a liar!"

"You're another."

"You're a lying coward and you don't dare stand up for yourself."

"Oh, get lost!"

"Listen—if you keep giving me any more of your smart mouth, I'll pick up a rock and throw it at your head."

"Oh, of course you will."

"Well I will."

"Well, why don't you just do it then? What's the point of constantly saying you will? Why aren't you taking action? It's because you're scared."

"I'm not afraid."

"You are."

"I'm not."

"You are."

Another pause followed, with more cautious glances and careful maneuvering around each other. Soon they found themselves standing shoulder to shoulder. Tom said:

"Get away from here!"

"Go away yourself!"

"I won't."

"I won't either."

So they stood there, each positioning one foot at an angle for support, both pushing with all their strength while glaring at each other with hatred. However, neither could gain the upper hand. After struggling until both were heated and red-faced, each eased up on their effort while remaining cautiously alert, and Tom said:

"You're a coward and a weakling. I'll tell my big brother on you, and he can beat you up with just his little finger, and I'll make sure he does it, too."

"What do I care about your big brother? I have a brother who's bigger than yours—and not only that, he can throw your brother right over that fence too." [Both brothers were imaginary.]

"That's a lie."

"Just because you say it doesn't make it true."

Tom drew a line in the dirt with his big toe and said:

"I challenge you to step over that line, and I'll beat you until you can't get back on your feet. Anyone who accepts a dare like that would steal sheep."

The new boy walked over right away and said:

"Now you said you'd do it, now let's see you do it."

"Don't crowd me right now; you'd better watch out."

"Well, you said you'd do it—why don't you do it?"

"By golly! For two cents I would do it."

The new boy pulled two large copper coins from his pocket and held them out mockingly. Tom knocked them to the ground. Instantly both boys were rolling and wrestling in the dirt, locked together like fighting cats; and for about a minute they pulled and ripped at each other's hair and clothing, punched and clawed at each other's faces, and covered themselves with dust and pride. Soon the chaos took shape, and through the haze of combat Tom emerged, sitting on top of the new boy and hitting him with his fists. "Say 'enough!'" he demanded.

The boy only fought to break free. He was crying—mostly from anger.

"Shout 'enough!'"—and the beating continued.

At last the stranger managed to get out a muffled "Enough!" and Tom let him up and said:

"That'll teach you a lesson. You better be careful about who you mess with next time."

The new boy walked away brushing the dirt from his clothes, crying, sniffling, and every now and then looking back and shaking his head while threatening what he would do to Tom the "next time he caught him." Tom responded with mocking laughter and walked off feeling proud of himself, but as soon as he turned his back, the new boy grabbed a stone, threw it, and struck him between the shoulder blades before turning around and running like a deer. Tom chased the coward all the way home and discovered where he lived. He then took up a position at the gate for quite a while, challenging his enemy to come outside, but his opponent only made faces at him through the window and refused to come out. Finally, the enemy's mother came out and called Tom a bad, mean, rude child, and told him to leave. So he left, but he said he planned to "wait" for that boy.

He arrived home quite late that evening, and when he carefully climbed through the window, he discovered a trap waiting for him in the form of his aunt; and when she saw the condition of his clothes, her decision to transform his Saturday holiday into imprisonment with hard work became unshakably firm.

Chapter II

Saturday morning had arrived, and the entire summer world was bright and fresh, overflowing with life. Every heart carried a song within it, and when that heart belonged to someone young, the music spilled from their lips. Joy filled every face and energy filled every step. The locust trees were blooming, and the sweet scent of their flowers drifted through the air. Cardiff Hill, which lay beyond and above the village, was lush with green plants and sat just far enough away to appear like a perfect paradise—dreamlike, peaceful, and welcoming.

Tom stepped onto the sidewalk carrying a bucket of whitewash and a long-handled brush. He looked at the fence, and all his happiness disappeared as a heavy sadness settled over him. Thirty yards of wooden fence, nine feet tall. Life felt empty to him, and living seemed like nothing but a burden. With a sigh, he dipped his brush and dragged it across the top board; he repeated the action; did it once more; compared the tiny whitewashed strip with the vast expanse of unpainted fence stretching before him, and sat down on a tree box, feeling defeated. Jim came bouncing out through the gate with a tin bucket, singing Buffalo Gals. Fetching water from the town pump had always seemed like terrible work to Tom before, but now it didn't seem so bad. He recalled that there was always company at the pump. White, mixed-race, and Black boys and girls were constantly gathered there waiting their turn, resting, swapping toys, arguing, fighting, and fooling around. And he remembered that even though the pump was only a hundred and fifty yards away, Jim never returned with a bucket of water in less than an hour—and even then someone usually had to go looking for him. Tom said:

"Listen, Jim, I'll go get the water if you'll do some of the whitewashing."

Jim shook his head and said:

"I can't, Tom. The old mistress told me I have to go get this water and not stop fooling around with anybody. She said she expects you're going to ask me to whitewash, so she told me to go along and take care of my own business—she said she'd take care of the whitewashing."

"Oh, don't worry about what she said, Jim. That's just how she always talks. Give me the bucket—I'll only be gone for a minute. She'll never know."

"Oh, I don't dare, Master Tom. Old mistress would take and tear my head clean off. Indeed she would."

"She! She never licks anybody—she just whacks them over the head with her thimble—and who cares about that, I'd like to know. She talks terribly, but talk doesn't hurt—at least it doesn't if she doesn't cry. Jim, I'll give you something amazing. I'll give you a white marble!"

Jim started to hesitate.

"What a perfect marble, Jim! And it's an excellent shooter."

"My! That's a really amazing marvel, I tell you! But Mars Tom I's powerfully afraid of old missis—"

"And besides, if you want, I'll show you my sore toe."

Jim was only human—this temptation was too strong for him to resist. He set down his bucket, accepted the white marble, and leaned over the injured toe with complete fascination while the bandage was being removed. Within seconds he was racing down the street carrying his bucket and nursing a stinging backside, Tom was painting the fence with renewed energy, and Aunt Polly was walking away from the scene with a slipper in her hand and victory gleaming in her eyes.

But Tom's energy didn't last long. He started thinking about all the fun activities he had planned for the day, and his sadness grew worse. Soon other kids who were free would come walking by, heading off on all kinds of exciting adventures, and they would make fun of him for having to work—just thinking about it made him feel like he was burning inside. He pulled out everything he owned and looked it over—small toy pieces, marbles, and other junk; maybe enough to trade for someone else to do some of the work, but nowhere near enough to buy even half an hour of complete freedom. So he put his limited possessions back in his pocket and abandoned the idea of trying to pay other boys to help him. At this dark and hopeless moment, a brilliant idea suddenly came to him! Nothing less than an absolutely amazing, wonderful inspiration.

He picked up his brush and calmly began to work. Ben Rogers appeared in the distance—the exact boy, of all the boys, whose mockery he had been fearing. Ben's walk was a hop-skip-and-jump—clear evidence that his spirits were high and his expectations bright. He was eating an apple and letting out long, musical whoops at regular intervals, followed by deep-toned ding-dong-dong, ding-dong-dong sounds, because he was pretending to be a steamboat. As he came closer, he slowed down, moved to the center of the street, leaned far over to the right and turned around heavily with elaborate ceremony—because he was pretending to be the Big Missouri and imagined himself drawing nine feet of water. He was the boat, captain, and engine bells all rolled into one, so he had to picture himself standing on his own upper deck giving orders and carrying them out:

"Stop her, sir! Ting-a-ling-ling!" The forward momentum nearly came to an end, and he pulled up gradually toward the curb.

"Ship up to back! Ting-a-ling-ling!" His arms straightened and became rigid at his sides.

"Turn her back to starboard! Ting-a-ling-ling! Chow! ch-chow-wow! Chow!" Meanwhile, his right hand traced grand, sweeping circles—since it was mimicking a forty-foot paddle wheel.

"Let her go back on the port side! Ting-a-ling-ling! Chow-ch-chow-chow!" The left hand began to trace circles in the air.

"Stop the starboard! Ting-a-ling-ling! Stop the larboard! Come ahead on the starboard! Stop her! Let your outside turn over slow! Ting-a-ling-ling! Chow-ow-ow! Get out that head-line! Lively now! Come—out with your spring-line—what are you doing there! Take a turn around that stump with the loop of it! Stand by that stage, now—let her go! Done with the engines, sir! Ting-a-ling-ling! SH'T! S'H'T! SH'T!" (trying the gauge-cocks).

Tom continued whitewashing—paying no attention to the steamboat. Ben stared for a moment and then said: "Hey! You're in a tough spot, aren't you!"

No response came. Tom examined his latest brushstroke with an artist's careful eye, then he made another smooth sweep with his brush and studied the outcome just as he had before. Ben walked up beside him. Tom's mouth began to water at the sight of the apple, but he continued with his task. Ben spoke:

"Hello, old friend, you have to work, right?"

Tom spun around suddenly and said:

"Oh, it's you, Ben! I wasn't paying attention."

"Hey—I'm going swimming, I am. Don't you wish you could? But of course you'd rather work—wouldn't you? Of course you would!"

Tom looked at the boy for a moment and said:

"What do you call work?"

"Why, isn't that work?"

Tom went back to whitewashing and replied casually:

"Well, maybe it is, and maybe it isn't. All I know is that it suits Tom Sawyer."

"Oh come on, you don't really mean to tell me that you actually like it?"

The brush kept moving.

"Like it? Well, I don't see why I shouldn't like it. Does a boy get a chance to whitewash a fence every day?"

That changed everything. Ben stopped eating his apple. Tom carefully moved his brush back and forth—stepped back to see how it looked—added a little touch here and there—looked at the results again—with Ben watching every movement and becoming more and more interested, more and more fascinated. Soon he said:

"Hey, Tom, let me do some whitewashing."

Tom thought about it and was ready to agree, but then he changed his mind:

"No—no—I don't think that would work, Ben. You see, Aunt Polly is extremely particular about this fence—right here on the street, you know—but if it were the back fence I wouldn't mind and she wouldn't either. Yes, she's extremely particular about this fence; it has to be done very carefully; I think there isn't one boy in a thousand, maybe two thousand, who can do it the way it needs to be done."

"No—is that really true? Oh come on now—let me just try it. Just for a little bit—I'd let you do it if you were me, Tom."

"Ben, I really would like to, I'm being honest with you; but Aunt Polly—well, Jim wanted to do it, but she wouldn't let him; Sid wanted to do it, and she wouldn't let Sid either. Now don't you see the position I'm in? If you were to take on this fence and something were to go wrong with it—"

"Oh, darn, I'll be just as careful. Now let me try. Hey—I'll give you the core of my apple."

"Well, here—No, Ben, don't do that. I'm afraid—"

"I'll give you all of it!"

Tom handed over the brush with reluctance showing on his face, but with eagerness filling his heart. And while the former steamboat Big Missouri labored and perspired under the sun, the retired artist perched on a barrel in the nearby shade, swinging his legs, eating his apple, and scheming to trick more unsuspecting victims. There was plenty of opportunity; boys wandered by regularly; they arrived to mock, but stayed to whitewash. By the time Ben was completely exhausted, Tom had exchanged the next turn to Billy Fisher for a kite in excellent condition; and when Billy was worn out, Johnny Miller purchased his chance for a dead rat and a string to swing it with—and this continued, hour after hour. And when the middle of the afternoon arrived, Tom had transformed from a poor, penniless boy that morning into someone literally overflowing with riches. Besides the items already mentioned, he possessed twelve marbles, part of a jew's harp, a piece of blue bottle glass for looking through, a spool cannon, a key that opened nothing, a piece of chalk, a glass stopper from a decanter, a tin soldier, a pair of tadpoles, six firecrackers, a one-eyed kitten, a brass doorknob, a dog collar—but no dog—a knife handle, four pieces of orange peel, and a worn-out old window frame.

He had enjoyed a wonderful, relaxing time the entire while—with plenty of friends around—and the fence now had three layers of whitewash on it! If he hadn't run out of whitewash, he would have taken every penny from every boy in the village.

Tom told himself that the world wasn't so empty and meaningless after all. Without realizing it, he had stumbled upon a fundamental principle of human behavior—that to make someone desperately want something, you simply need to make it hard to get. If he had been a brilliant philosopher like the author of this book, he would have understood that work is anything a person has to do, while play is anything a person doesn't have to do. This insight would have helped him grasp why making artificial flowers or running on a treadmill counts as work, while bowling or mountain climbing is just fun. There are rich men in England who spend their summers driving four-horse passenger coaches twenty or thirty miles every day along regular routes, paying handsomely for the privilege; but if someone offered to pay them wages for doing the exact same thing, it would become work and they would quit immediately.

The boy thought for a while about the major change that had occurred in his life situation, and then headed toward headquarters to report.

Chapter III

Tom appeared before Aunt Polly, who was sitting by an open window in a cozy back room that served as bedroom, breakfast room, dining room, and library all rolled into one. The gentle summer breeze, the peaceful silence, the scent of flowers, and the sleepy humming of bees had worked their magic, and she was dozing off over her knitting—since her only companion was the cat, which lay sleeping in her lap. Her glasses were pushed up onto her gray hair for safekeeping. She had assumed that Tom had surely run off long ago, and she was surprised to see him boldly put himself back within her reach like this. He said: "May I go play now, aunt?"

"What, already? How much have you done?"

"It's all finished, aunt."

"Tom, don't lie to me—I can't stand it."

"I'm not, aunt; it's all finished."

Aunt Polly didn't put much faith in that kind of proof. She went outside to check for herself, and she would have been satisfied to discover that even twenty percent of Tom's story was accurate. When she saw the whole fence painted white, and not just painted but carefully covered with multiple coats, and even a line painted on the ground, her amazement was nearly beyond words. She said:

"Well, I'll be! There's no denying it—you can work when you set your mind to it, Tom." Then she weakened the compliment by adding, "But you rarely set your mind to it, I have to say. Well, go on and play, but make sure you come back sometime this week, or I'll give you a beating."

She was so overwhelmed by the magnificence of what he had accomplished that she led him into the pantry and picked out a perfect apple, giving it to him along with an uplifting speech about how much more valuable and delicious a reward becomes when it's earned through honest, virtuous work rather than obtained through wrongdoing. And while she concluded her remarks with a joyful biblical quotation, he secretly snatched a doughnut.

Then he darted outside and spotted Sid beginning to climb the outdoor staircase that led to the back rooms on the upper floor. Dirt clods were within easy reach, and the air was filled with them in an instant. They pelted Sid like a fierce hailstorm, and before Aunt Polly could gather her startled wits and rush to help, six or seven clods had found their mark, and Tom had vaulted over the fence and disappeared. There was a gate available, but he was usually in too much of a hurry to bother using it. His mind was at ease now that he had gotten even with Sid for drawing attention to his black thread and landing him in trouble.

Tom walked around the block and entered a muddy alley that ran behind his aunt's cow barn. He soon reached a safe distance where he couldn't be caught or punished, and hurried toward the town's public square, where two "military" companies of boys had arranged to meet for battle. Tom served as General of one of these armies, while Joe Harper, a close friend, commanded the other. These two great leaders didn't lower themselves to fight directly—that was more appropriate for the younger boys—but instead sat together on a hill and directed the battlefield operations by giving orders through their assistants. Tom's army achieved a decisive victory after a lengthy and fiercely contested battle. Afterward, they counted the casualties, traded prisoners, settled the terms of their next conflict, and scheduled the date for the upcoming battle; then the armies formed ranks and marched away, leaving Tom to walk home by himself.

As he walked past Jeff Thatcher's house, he spotted a new girl in the garden—a beautiful little blue-eyed girl with blonde hair braided into two long pigtails, wearing a white summer dress and decorated underwear. The newly victorious hero was defeated without putting up any fight. A certain Amy Lawrence disappeared from his heart and left not even a trace of herself behind. He had believed he loved her desperately; he had considered his feelings to be deep devotion; and suddenly it turned out to be nothing more than a weak little temporary attraction. He had spent months trying to win her over; she had admitted her feelings just a week ago; he had been the happiest and most proud boy in the world only seven short days ago, and now in a single moment she had left his heart like a random visitor whose stay had ended.

He admired this new angel with secretive glances until he realized she had noticed him; then he acted as if he didn't know she was there and started showing off in all kinds of ridiculous boyish ways to win her admiration. He continued this silly behavior for a while; but eventually, while he was in the middle of some risky acrobatic stunts, he looked over and saw that the little girl was making her way toward the house. Tom walked up to the fence and leaned against it, feeling sad and hoping she would stay a little longer. She paused for a moment on the steps and then headed toward the door. Tom let out a deep sigh as she stepped onto the threshold. But his face brightened immediately, because she threw a pansy over the fence just before she vanished.

The boy ran around and came to a stop just a foot or two away from the flower, then shielded his eyes with his hand and started looking down the street as though he had spotted something interesting happening in that direction. Soon he picked up a piece of straw and started attempting to balance it on his nose, tilting his head far back; as he swayed from side to side in his attempts, he gradually moved closer and closer to the pansy; eventually his bare foot came to rest on it, his flexible toes curled around it, and he hopped away with his prize and vanished around the corner. But he was gone for only a moment—just long enough to tuck the flower inside his jacket, close to his heart—or perhaps near his stomach, since he wasn't well-versed in anatomy and wasn't particularly concerned about such details anyway.

He came back and lingered around the fence until dark, showing off just like before, but the girl didn't appear again, though Tom found some comfort in hoping that she might have been watching from a window somewhere and had noticed his efforts to impress her. Eventually he walked home with reluctance, his mind filled with dreams of her.

Throughout dinner, he was in such high spirits that his aunt wondered "what had gotten into the boy." He received a thorough scolding for throwing dirt clods at Sid, but it didn't seem to bother him at all. He attempted to sneak sugar right under his aunt's nose and got his knuckles smacked for it. He said:

"Aunt, you don't hit Sid when he takes it."

"Well, Sid doesn't torment a person the way you do. You'd always be getting into that sugar if I wasn't watching you."

Soon she walked into the kitchen, and Sid, feeling safe from punishment, reached for the sugar bowl—a kind of triumph over Tom that was almost too much to bear. But Sid's fingers slipped and the bowl fell and shattered. Tom was thrilled beyond words. He was so excited that he even kept his mouth shut and stayed quiet. He told himself that he wouldn't say a single word, even when his aunt returned, but would sit completely still until she asked who had caused the trouble; and then he would tell her, and nothing in the world would be better than watching that perfect little angel "get what's coming to him." He was so filled with joy that he could barely contain himself when the old woman came back and stood over the broken pieces, shooting angry looks from behind her glasses. He thought to himself, "Here it comes!" And the next moment he was flat on the floor! Her powerful hand was raised to hit again when Tom shouted:

"Wait a minute, why are you hitting me?—Sid's the one who broke it!"

Aunt Polly stopped, confused, and Tom hoped for some comforting sympathy. But when she found her voice again, she simply said:

"Ugh! Well, I don't think you got punished unfairly at all. You've probably been up to some other bold mischief when I wasn't around, most likely."

Then her conscience troubled her, and she longed to say something kind and loving; but she believed that this would be interpreted as an admission that she had been wrong, and proper discipline prevented that. So she remained silent, and went about her daily tasks with a heavy heart. Tom pouted in a corner and magnified his troubles. He knew that in her heart his aunt was pleading with him, and he was grimly satisfied by this awareness. He would send out no peace offerings, he would acknowledge none. He knew that longing looks fell upon him from time to time, through a veil of tears, but he refused to acknowledge them. He imagined himself lying deathly ill with his aunt leaning over him, begging for one small word of forgiveness, but he would turn his face to the wall and die with that word unspoken. Oh, how would she feel then? And he imagined himself carried home from the river, dead, with his hair all wet, and his aching heart finally at peace. How she would throw herself upon him, and how her tears would fall like rain, and her lips would beg God to bring back her boy and she would never, never mistreat him again! But he would lie there cold and pale and give no response—a poor little victim, whose suffering had ended. He worked himself up so much with the sadness of these fantasies that he had to keep swallowing to avoid choking; and his eyes filled with tears, which spilled over when he blinked, and ran down and dripped from the tip of his nose. And such a pleasure it was for him to nurture his sorrows, that he could not stand to have any ordinary happiness or jarring joy interfere with it; it was too precious for such interruption; and so, soon after, when his cousin Mary danced in, bursting with the happiness of seeing home again after what felt like an endless visit of one week to the country, he got up and moved in gloom and shadow out one door as she brought music and brightness in through the other.

He wandered far from the usual places where boys spent their time, seeking out lonely spots that matched his mood. A log raft floating in the river caught his attention, and he sat down on its edge, staring at the gloomy expanse of water while wishing he could simply drown all at once without awareness, avoiding the unpleasant process that nature had designed. Then his thoughts turned to his flower. He pulled it out, now crumpled and withered, and it greatly deepened his melancholy satisfaction. He wondered whether she would feel sorry for him if she knew about his situation. Would she weep and wish she had the right to wrap her arms around his neck and console him? Or would she turn away coldly like everyone else in this heartless world? This mental image brought such intense bittersweet pain that he replayed it repeatedly in his thoughts, examining it from different angles until he had exhausted every detail. Finally, he stood up with a sigh and walked away into the night.

Around nine-thirty or ten o'clock, he walked down the empty street to where his Beloved Unknown lived. He stopped for a moment, listening carefully, but heard nothing. A candle cast a dim light through the curtains of a second-floor window. Was she there in that sacred place? He climbed over the fence and quietly made his way through the garden plants until he stood beneath her window. He gazed up at it for a long time, filled with deep emotion. Then he lay down on the ground underneath it, positioning himself on his back with his hands folded across his chest, clutching his poor withered flower. This is how he would die—alone in the harsh world, with no roof over his head, no kind hand to wipe away the sweat of death from his forehead, no loving face to look down on him with compassion during his final moments. This is how she would find him when she looked out into the bright morning, and oh! Would she shed even one small tear for his poor, lifeless body? Would she let out even one small sigh upon seeing such a promising young life so cruelly destroyed, so tragically ended before its time?

The window shot up, a maid's harsh voice shattered the sacred silence, and a flood of water soaked the fallen martyr's body!

The choking hero jumped up with a relieved snort. There was a whistling sound like a projectile cutting through the air, mixed with the mumble of a curse, followed by the sound of shattering glass, and a small, unclear figure went over the fence and disappeared quickly into the darkness.

Not long after, as Tom stood undressed for bed, examining his soaked clothes by the light of a candle, Sid woke up; but if he had any vague notion of making any hints or comments, he reconsidered and kept quiet, because he could see the dangerous look in Tom's eyes.

Tom went to bed without the extra annoyance of saying his prayers, and Sid mentally noted that he had skipped them.

Chapter IV

The sun rose over a peaceful world and shone down on the quiet village like a blessing. After breakfast, Aunt Polly led the family in worship: it started with a prayer constructed entirely from solid blocks of Biblical quotations, held together with just a thin layer of her own words; and from the peak of this foundation she delivered a stern chapter from the Law of Moses, as if speaking from Mount Sinai itself.

Then Tom prepared himself, so to speak, and got down to work to "learn his verses." Sid had already memorized his lesson days earlier. Tom focused all his effort on memorizing five verses, and he selected a portion of the Sermon on the Mount because he couldn't find any verses that were shorter. After half an hour, Tom had only a rough general understanding of his lesson, and nothing more, since his mind was wandering across every possible topic, and his hands were occupied with various distractions. Mary took his book to listen to him recite, and he attempted to navigate through the confusion:

"Blessed are the—a—a—"

"Poor"—

"Yes—poor; blessed are the poor—a—a—"

"In spirit—"

"In spirit; blessed are the poor in spirit, for they—they—"

"Theirs—"

"For theirs. Blessed are the poor in spirit, for theirs is the kingdom of heaven. Blessed are those who mourn, for they—they—"

"Sh—"

"For they—a—"

"S, H, A—"

"For they S, H—Oh, I don't know what it is!"

"Shall!"

"Oh, shall! for they shall—for they shall—a—a—shall mourn—a—a—blessed are they that shall—they that—a—they that shall mourn, for they shall—a—shall what? Why don't you tell me, Mary?—what do you want to be so mean for?"

"Oh, Tom, you poor confused thing, I'm not making fun of you. I would never do that. You need to go and study it again. Don't get discouraged, Tom, you'll figure it out—and when you do, I'll give you something really wonderful. There, now, that's a good boy."

"All right! What is it, Mary, tell me what it is."

"Don't worry about it, Tom. You know that when I say something is nice, it really is nice."

"You can bet that's true, Mary. All right, I'll give it another try."

And he did "tackle it again"—and under the double pressure of curiosity and potential profit, he approached it with such enthusiasm that he achieved a brilliant success. Mary gave him a brand-new "Barlow" knife worth twelve and a half cents; and the wave of joy that flooded through him shook him to his core. Admittedly, the knife wouldn't cut anything, but it was a genuine Barlow, and there was unimaginable magnificence in that—though where the Western boys ever developed the notion that such a tool could possibly be faked to its detriment remains a puzzling mystery and probably always will. Tom managed to scratch up the cupboard with it, and was planning to start on the dresser, when he was summoned to get dressed for Sunday school.

Mary handed him a metal washbasin filled with water and a bar of soap, and he stepped outside the door and placed the basin on a small bench that was there; then he dunked the soap into the water and set it aside; rolled up his sleeves; carefully poured the water onto the ground, and then walked into the kitchen and started thoroughly wiping his face with the towel hanging behind the door. However, Mary took the towel away and said:

"Aren't you ashamed, Tom? You shouldn't be so difficult. Water won't hurt you."

Tom felt a bit unsettled. The basin was filled again, and this time he stood over it for a moment, building up his courage; he took a deep breath and started. When he walked into the kitchen shortly after, with both eyes closed and feeling around for the towel with his hands, soap suds and water were dripping from his face as proof of his efforts. But when he came out from behind the towel, the result still wasn't good enough, because the clean area only went down to his chin and jawline, like a mask; below and beyond this point there was a dark stretch of unwashed skin that extended downward across his front and back around his neck. Mary took charge of him, and when she finished with him he was clean all over, without any difference in color, and his soaked hair was neatly combed, with its short curls arranged into an attractive and balanced overall look. [He secretly smoothed out the curls, working hard and struggling with them, and flattened his hair down against his head; because he thought curls were feminine, and his own made his life miserable.] Then Mary brought out a set of his clothes that had only been worn on Sundays for two years—they were simply called his "other clothes"—and this tells us how limited his wardrobe was. The girl "fixed him up" after he had gotten dressed; she buttoned his nice jacket all the way up to his chin, folded his large shirt collar down over his shoulders, brushed him clean and topped him off with his spotted straw hat. He now looked much better and very uncomfortable. He felt just as uncomfortable as he appeared; because there was something restrictive about good clothes and being clean that bothered him. He hoped that Mary would forget about his shoes, but that hope was crushed; she covered them completely with grease, as was the usual practice, and brought them out. He became angry and said he was always being forced to do everything he didn't want to do.

But Mary said, in a convincing way:

"Please, Tom—that's a good boy."

So he put on the shoes while grumbling angrily. Mary was ready quickly, and the three children headed out for Sunday school—a place that Tom despised completely; but Sid and Mary enjoyed it.

Sabbath-school hours ran from nine to half-past ten, followed by church service. Two of the children always stayed for the sermon by choice, while the other always stayed as well—though for more compelling reasons. The church's tall-backed, uncushioned pews could accommodate roughly three hundred people; the building was simply a small, modest structure with what looked like a pine board tree-box serving as a steeple on top. At the entrance, Tom stepped back and approached a friend dressed in Sunday clothes:

"Hey, Billy, do you have a yellow ticket?"

"Yes."

"What will you take for her?"

"What will you give?"

"Piece of licorice and a fishhook."

"Let's see them."

Tom displayed his tickets. They were acceptable, and the exchange was completed. Then Tom traded a couple of white marbles for three red tickets, and some small item for a pair of blue ones. He intercepted other boys as they arrived, and continued purchasing tickets of different colors for ten or fifteen minutes more. He entered the church now, accompanied by a crowd of clean and loud boys and girls, walked to his seat and began a fight with the first boy within reach. The teacher, a serious, older man, stepped in; then turned away briefly and Tom yanked a boy's hair from the bench behind him, and was engrossed in his book when the boy looked back; poked a pin into another boy shortly after, hoping to hear him cry "Ouch!" and received another scolding from his teacher. Tom's entire class followed the same pattern—fidgety, loud, and disruptive. When the time came to recite their lessons, none of them knew their verses completely, but required prompting throughout. Nevertheless, they managed to get through it, and each received his reward—small blue tickets, each containing a Bible verse; each blue ticket served as payment for two recited verses. Ten blue tickets equaled one red ticket, and could be traded for it; ten red tickets equaled one yellow ticket; for ten yellow tickets the superintendent awarded a very simply bound Bible (worth forty cents in those simpler times) to the student. How many of my readers would possess the dedication and effort to memorize two thousand verses, even for a Doré Bible? Yet Mary had earned two Bibles this way—it represented the patient effort of two years—and a boy of German heritage had earned four or five. He once recited three thousand verses without pause; but the pressure on his mind was too severe, and he remained little more than a simpleton from that moment on—a terrible loss for the school, because on special occasions, in front of visitors, the superintendent (as Tom put it) had always brought this boy forward to "show off." Only the older students succeeded in keeping their tickets and persisting with their boring work long enough to earn a Bible, so the awarding of one of these prizes was an unusual and significant event; the winning student became so important and prominent for that day that immediately every student's heart was inspired with a new ambition that frequently lasted several weeks. It's likely that Tom's mind had never truly craved one of those prizes, but undoubtedly his whole spirit had for many days yearned for the fame and recognition that accompanied it.

Eventually the superintendent rose to his feet in front of the pulpit, holding a closed hymn-book with his finger marking a place between the pages, and called for everyone's attention. Whenever a Sunday-school superintendent delivers his usual brief speech, carrying a hymn-book is just as essential as a singer holding sheet music when stepping forward on stage to perform a solo at a concert—though the reason remains unclear, since neither the hymn-book nor the sheet music is actually consulted by the person using it. This superintendent was a thin man of thirty-five years, sporting a sandy-colored goatee and short sandy hair; he was dressed in a rigid upright collar that nearly touched his ears, with sharp points that curved forward alongside the corners of his mouth—creating a barrier that forced him to look straight ahead and required him to turn his entire body whenever he needed to glance sideways; his chin rested on an expansive necktie that was as wide and long as a banknote, complete with fringed edges; his boot tips curved sharply upward in the style of that era, resembling sleigh runners—a look that young men achieved through the patient and tedious process of sitting with their toes pressed against a wall for hours at a time. Mr. Walters possessed a very serious demeanor and maintained a genuinely sincere and honest character; he regarded sacred things and places with such deep respect, keeping them so distinctly separate from secular concerns, that without realizing it, his Sunday-school speaking voice had developed a distinctive tone that was completely absent during weekdays. He started speaking in this manner:

"Now, children, I want you all to sit up as straight and nicely as you can and give me your complete attention for a minute or two. There—that's it. That's how good little boys and girls should behave. I see one little girl who is looking out the window—I'm afraid she thinks I'm out there somewhere—maybe up in one of the trees giving a speech to the little birds. [Appreciative giggling.] I want to tell you how wonderful it makes me feel to see so many bright, clean little faces gathered in a place like this, learning to do what's right and be good." And so on and so forth. It isn't necessary to write down the rest of the speech. It followed a pattern that never changes, and so we're all familiar with it.

The final third of the speech was disrupted by renewed fighting and other distractions among some of the troublemakers, and by restless movements and whispered conversations that spread throughout the room, reaching even the most well-behaved and reliable students like Sid and Mary. But then every noise stopped abruptly when Mr. Walters' voice faded away, and the end of the speech was met with an explosion of silent relief.

Much of the whispering had been caused by something that didn't happen very often—the arrival of visitors: lawyer Thatcher, along with a very frail and elderly man; a handsome, well-built, middle-aged gentleman with iron-gray hair; and a distinguished lady who was clearly the latter's wife. The lady was guiding a child. Tom had been restless and filled with irritation and complaints; guilt-ridden, too—he couldn't look Amy Lawrence in the eye, he couldn't stand her affectionate gaze. But when he spotted this small newcomer his spirit was instantly set on fire with joy. The next moment he was "showing off" with everything he had—hitting boys, yanking hair, making silly expressions—in short, using every trick that might captivate a girl and earn her admiration. His excitement had only one flaw—the memory of his embarrassment in this angel's garden—and that mark in the sand was quickly being erased, washed away by the waves of happiness that were now flooding over it.

The visitors received the most honored seats, and once Mr. Walters finished his speech, he presented them to the school. The middle-aged man proved to be an extraordinary figure—none other than the county judge—the most distinguished person these children had ever seen—and they wondered what he was made of—and they partly wanted to hear him speak loudly, while also being somewhat afraid he might. He came from Constantinople, twelve miles away—so he had traveled and experienced the world—those very eyes had gazed upon the county courthouse—which was rumored to have a tin roof. The wonder that these thoughts created was shown by the remarkable silence and rows of wide-eyed stares. This was the great Judge Thatcher, brother of their own lawyer. Jeff Thatcher quickly stepped forward to become acquainted with the important man and earn the envy of the school. It would have been like music to his ears to hear the whispered conversations:

"Look at him, Jim! He's going up there. Hey—look! He's going to shake hands with him—he is shaking hands with him! Wow, don't you wish you were Jeff?"

Mr. Walters began putting on a show, bustling around with all kinds of official activities, barking out orders, making judgments, and giving directions here, there, and everywhere he could find someone to target. The librarian put on his own display—rushing back and forth with his arms loaded with books, creating the kind of commotion and fuss that petty authority figures love. The young female teachers showed off by sweetly bending over students they had recently been scolding, raising pretty warning fingers at misbehaving little boys and lovingly patting the well-behaved ones. The young male teachers displayed their authority through minor reprimands and other small demonstrations of power and careful attention to discipline—and most of the teachers, both men and women, discovered they had urgent business near the library by the pulpit, business that often needed to be repeated two or three times with much apparent frustration. The little girls showed off in different ways, while the little boys performed with such enthusiasm that the air grew thick with paper balls and the sounds of scuffling. Above all this commotion, the distinguished visitor sat beaming with a grand, dignified smile at the entire gathering, basking in the warmth of his own importance—because he was showing off as well.

There was only one thing missing to make Mr. Walters completely overjoyed, and that was an opportunity to present a Bible prize and showcase a remarkable student. Several students had a few yellow tickets, but none had collected enough—he had gone around asking all the top students. He would have given anything now to have that German boy back again with his mind intact.

And now at this moment, when hope was dead, Tom Sawyer came forward with nine yellow tickets, nine red tickets, and ten blue ones, and demanded a Bible. This was a thunderbolt out of a clear sky. Walters wasn't expecting an application from this source for the next ten years. But there was no way around it—here were the certified checks, and they were good for their face value. Tom was therefore elevated to a place with the Judge and the other chosen ones, and the great news was announced from headquarters. It was the most stunning surprise of the decade, and so profound was the sensation that it lifted the new hero up to the judicial one's level, and the school had two marvels to gaze upon instead of one. The boys were all consumed with envy—but those who suffered the most bitter pangs were those who realized too late that they themselves had contributed to this hated splendor by trading tickets to Tom for the wealth he had accumulated in selling whitewashing privileges. These boys despised themselves, seeing themselves as the victims of a cunning fraud, a deceitful snake in the grass.

The prize was given to Tom with all the enthusiasm the superintendent could manage under the circumstances, but it fell short of genuine excitement. The poor man's instincts told him there was something mysterious going on that probably wouldn't hold up under scrutiny. It was absolutely ridiculous to think this boy had actually stored two thousand pieces of Biblical knowledge in his head—a dozen would likely push his limits, without question.

Amy Lawrence felt proud and happy, and she tried to let Tom see these feelings in her expression—but he refused to look at her. She felt puzzled; then she became slightly worried; next a vague suspicion appeared and disappeared—then returned again; she kept watching; a secretive look revealed everything to her—and then her heart shattered, and she felt jealous, and furious, and tears began to flow and she despised everyone. She hated Tom more than anyone else (she believed).

Tom was introduced to the Judge, but he couldn't speak, could barely breathe, and his heart was pounding—partly because of the man's intimidating presence, but mostly because he was her father. Tom would have gladly fallen to his knees and worshipped him if no one could see. The Judge placed his hand on Tom's head and called him a fine young man, then asked what his name was. The boy stuttered, struggled for breath, and finally managed to get it out:

"Tom."

"Oh, no, not Tom—it is—"

"Thomas."

"Oh, that's it. I thought there might be more to it, perhaps. That's fine. But I'm sure you have another one, and you'll share it with me, won't you?"

"Tell the gentleman what your other name is, Thomas," Walters said, "and remember to say sir. You can't forget your manners."

"Thomas Sawyer—sir."

"That's it! That's a good boy. Fine boy. Fine, manly little fellow. Two thousand verses is a great many—very, very great many. And you can never regret the effort you put into learning them; because knowledge is worth more than anything else in the world; it's what creates great men and good men; you'll become a great man and a good man yourself someday, Thomas, and then you'll look back and say, It's all because of the valuable Sunday-school opportunities of my childhood—it's all because of my wonderful teachers who taught me to learn—it's all because of the good superintendent, who encouraged me, and looked after me, and gave me a beautiful Bible—a magnificent elegant Bible—to keep and have it all for myself, always—it's all because of proper upbringing! That is what you will say, Thomas—and you wouldn't accept any money for those two thousand verses—no indeed you wouldn't. And now you wouldn't mind sharing with me and this lady some of the things you've learned—no, I know you wouldn't—because we are proud of little boys who learn. Now, I'm sure you know the names of all the twelve disciples. Won't you tell us the names of the first two who were chosen?"

Tom was pulling at a buttonhole and looking embarrassed. He turned red now, and his gaze dropped. Mr. Walters felt his heart sink. He thought to himself that there was no way the boy could answer even the most basic question—why had the Judge asked him? Still, he felt he had to speak up and say:

"Answer the gentleman, Thomas—don't be afraid."

Tom still hesitated.

"Now I know you'll tell me," the lady said. "The names of the first two disciples were—"

"David and Goliath!"

Let us draw the curtain of charity over the rest of the scene.

Chapter V

Around ten-thirty, the cracked bell of the small church started ringing, and soon people began gathering for the morning service. The Sunday school children spread themselves throughout the building and sat in pews with their parents to stay under watchful eyes. Aunt Polly arrived, and Tom, Sid, and Mary sat beside her—with Tom positioned next to the aisle so he would be as far as possible from the open window and the tempting summer scenes outside. The congregation filled the aisles: the elderly and struggling postmaster who had known better times; the mayor and his wife—since they had a mayor there, among other unnecessary officials; the justice of the peace; the widow Douglas, attractive, sharp, and forty years old, a kind-hearted and generous woman who was well-off, whose hilltop mansion was the town's only grand house and the most welcoming and extravagant when it came to entertaining that St. Petersburg could claim; the stooped and respected Major and Mrs. Ward; lawyer Riverson, the new distinguished visitor from out of town; then the village beauty, followed by a group of young women dressed in white lawn fabric and decorated with ribbons who broke hearts wherever they went; after that came all the young store clerks in town as a group—since they had lingered in the entrance hall chewing on their walking stick handles, forming a circle of slicked-down hair and foolish grins around the admirers, until the last girl had passed through their gauntlet; and finally came the Model Boy, Willie Mufferson, taking such careful attention of his mother as if she were made of delicate crystal. He always escorted his mother to church and was the favorite of all the older women. All the boys despised him because he was so well-behaved. Moreover, he had been held up as an example to them constantly. His white handkerchief was sticking out of his back pocket, as it always was on Sundays—supposedly by accident. Tom didn't have a handkerchief, and he considered boys who carried them to be show-offs.

The congregation was now fully gathered, and the bell rang one final time to alert any latecomers and those still arriving, after which a reverent silence settled over the church that was interrupted only by the giggling and murmuring of the choir up in the gallery. The choir always giggled and murmured throughout the entire service. There was once a church choir that displayed proper manners, but I have now forgotten where that was. It happened many years ago, and I can barely recall any details about it, though I believe it was in some foreign country.

The minister announced the hymn and read it aloud with great enthusiasm, using a distinctive style that was highly praised in that region. His voice started at a moderate pitch and gradually rose until it reached a specific point, where it emphasized the highest word with powerful force before dropping down sharply as if diving from a springboard:

Shall I be carried to the skies on flowery beds of ease, while others fight to win the prize and sail through bloody seas?

He was considered an exceptional reader. At church social gatherings, people always asked him to recite poetry, and when he finished, the women would raise their hands and drop them limply into their laps, roll their eyes dramatically, and shake their heads, as if to say, "There are no words to describe it; it's too beautiful, TOO beautiful for this world."

After the hymn was finished, Reverend Mr. Sprague transformed himself into a human announcement board and began reading out notices about meetings, societies, and various other events until it felt like the list might go on forever—a strange tradition that continues in America even today, including in cities, despite our era of plentiful newspapers. Frequently, the less reason there is for keeping a traditional custom alive, the more difficult it becomes to eliminate it.

And now the minister prayed. It was a good, generous prayer that went into great detail: it pleaded for the church and the little children of the church; for the other churches in the village; for the village itself; for the county; for the state; for the state officers; for the United States; for the churches of the United States; for Congress; for the President; for the officers of the government; for poor sailors being tossed about by stormy seas; for the oppressed millions suffering under the rule of European monarchies and Oriental despotisms; for those who have the light and the good news, yet do not have eyes to see or ears to hear; for the heathens on the distant islands of the sea; and concluded with a request that the words he was about to speak might find grace and favor, and be like seed planted in fertile soil, producing in time a grateful harvest of good. Amen.

There was a rustling of dresses, and the standing congregation sat down. The boy whose story this book tells didn't enjoy the prayer—he simply endured it, if he even managed that much. He fidgeted throughout the entire thing, unconsciously keeping track of every detail of the prayer since he wasn't really listening, but he knew the familiar territory and the minister's usual path through it. When some small bit of new content was added, his ear caught it and his entire being rebelled against it; he thought such additions were unfair and dishonest. During the prayer, a fly had landed on the back of the pew in front of him and tormented his spirit by calmly rubbing its hands together, wrapping its arms around its head, and polishing it so energetically that it seemed ready to separate from its body, revealing the thin thread of its neck. The fly scraped its wings with its back legs and smoothed them against its body as if they were coat-tails, going through its entire grooming routine as peacefully as if it knew it was completely safe. And indeed it was, because even though Tom's hands were itching terribly to grab it, he didn't dare—he believed his soul would be immediately destroyed if he did such a thing while the prayer was happening. But as the closing sentence began, his hand started to curve and creep forward, and the moment "Amen" was spoken, the fly became a prisoner of war. His aunt noticed what he'd done and made him release it.

The minister announced his text and droned on monotonously through an argument that was so dull that many heads gradually began to nod—yet it was an argument that spoke of endless fire and brimstone and narrowed down the predestined elect to a group so small it was hardly worth saving. Tom counted the pages of the sermon; after church he always knew how many pages there had been, but he rarely knew anything else about the speech. However, this time he was genuinely interested for a brief while. The minister painted a grand and moving picture of the gathering of the world's armies at the millennium when the lion and the lamb would lie down together and a little child would lead them. But the emotion, the lesson, the moral of the great spectacle were lost on the boy; he only thought about how prominent the main character would be before the watching nations; his face brightened with the thought, and he told himself that he wished he could be that child, if it was a tame lion.

Now he fell back into boredom as the dry sermon continued. Soon he remembered a treasure he owned and pulled it out. It was a large black beetle with intimidating jaws—he called it a "pinchbug." He kept it in a small metal box. The first thing the beetle did was bite his finger. He naturally flicked it away, sending the beetle tumbling into the aisle where it landed on its back, and he stuck his hurt finger in his mouth. The beetle lay there wiggling its helpless legs, unable to flip over. Tom stared at it and wanted it back, but it was safely beyond his reach. Other people who weren't paying attention to the sermon also found entertainment in watching the beetle. Soon a stray poodle wandered by, feeling sad and sluggish from the warm summer air and the quiet atmosphere, tired of being confined and yearning for something exciting. He noticed the beetle; his drooping tail perked up and started wagging. He examined his discovery, walked in circles around it, sniffed it from a safe distance, circled it again, became braver and took a closer sniff, then curled his lip and carefully tried to grab it, barely missing; he tried again and again, starting to enjoy the entertainment. He lay down on his belly with the beetle between his paws and kept experimenting with it. Eventually he grew tired and then lost interest and became distracted. His head began to droop, and gradually his chin lowered until it touched his enemy, who immediately clamped down on it. There was a sharp cry, the poodle jerked his head, and the beetle flew a few yards away, landing on its back again. The nearby onlookers trembled with quiet amusement, several faces disappeared behind fans and handkerchiefs, and Tom felt completely delighted. The dog looked embarrassed and probably felt that way too, but he also harbored resentment and a desire for payback. So he approached the beetle and launched another cautious assault, leaping at it from all angles, landing with his front paws just inches from the creature, making even closer attempts to grab it with his teeth, and shaking his head so hard his ears flapped wildly. But after a while he became tired again; he tried to entertain himself with a fly but found no satisfaction; he followed an ant around with his nose pressed to the floor and quickly lost interest in that too; he yawned, sighed, completely forgot about the beetle, and sat down directly on top of it. Then came a piercing howl of pain and the poodle shot up the aisle; the yelping continued, and so did the dog's frantic movement; he raced across the front of the church near the altar; he flew down the opposite aisle; he dashed past the entrance doors; he scrambled up the center aisle; his suffering intensified with each movement, until soon he became like a furry comet streaking through its path with brilliant speed. Finally the panicked animal veered off course and leaped into his owner's lap; the man threw him out the window, and the sounds of distress quickly faded and disappeared into the distance.

By this time the entire church was red-faced and choking back their laughter, and the sermon had completely stopped. The preaching continued after a moment, but it was awkward and stumbling, with no chance of being impressive anymore; even the most serious statements kept getting quiet bursts of inappropriate laughter from behind distant pews, as if the poor minister had said something incredibly funny. The whole congregation felt genuinely relieved when the ordeal ended and the benediction was given.

Tom Sawyer walked home feeling quite happy, thinking that church service could actually be satisfying when it had some excitement mixed in. Only one thing bothered him about what had happened; he didn't mind that the dog had played with his beetle, but he didn't think it was right for the dog to have taken it away.

Chapter VI

Monday morning left Tom Sawyer feeling miserable. Every Monday morning had the same effect on him—it marked the start of another week of tedious suffering at school. He usually started the day wishing there had been no weekend break at all, since it made returning to what felt like imprisonment and chains so much more unbearable.

Tom lay there thinking. Soon it occurred to him that he wished he was sick; then he could stay home from school. Here was a vague possibility. He examined his body. No illness was found, and he investigated again. This time he thought he could detect stomach pain symptoms, and he began to encourage them with considerable hope. But they soon grew weak, and soon died away completely. He thought further. Suddenly he discovered something. One of his upper front teeth was loose. This was fortunate; he was about to begin groaning, as a "starter," as he called it, when it occurred to him that if he came into court with that argument, his aunt would pull it out, and that would hurt. So he thought he would keep the tooth in reserve for now, and look further. Nothing presented itself for some time, and then he remembered hearing the doctor talk about a certain condition that kept a patient bedridden for two or three weeks and threatened to make him lose a finger. So the boy eagerly pulled his sore toe from under the sheet and held it up for examination. But now he did not know the necessary symptoms. However, it seemed well worth trying, so he began groaning with considerable energy.

But Sid continued sleeping, completely unaware.

Tom groaned more loudly and imagined that he was starting to feel pain in his toe.

No response from Sid.

Tom was breathing heavily from all his hard work by this point. He paused to catch his breath, then puffed himself up and let out a series of impressive groans.

Sid kept snoring.

Tom was frustrated. He called out, "Sid, Sid!" and shook him. This approach worked effectively, and Tom started groaning once more. Sid yawned, stretched his body, then propped himself up on his elbow with a snort, and began staring at Tom. Tom continued his groaning. Sid said:

"Tom! Hey, Tom!" [No response.] "Come here, Tom! TOM! What's wrong, Tom?" And he shook him and looked at his face with concern.

Tom let out a moan:

"Oh, don't, Sid. Don't shake me."

"What's wrong, Tom? I need to call auntie."

"No—never mind. It'll be over soon, maybe. Don't call anybody."

"But I have to! Stop groaning like that, Tom, it's terrible. How long have you been like this?"

"Hours. Ouch! Oh, don't move around so much, Sid, you'll kill me."

"Tom, why didn't you wake me up earlier? Oh, Tom, stop! It makes my skin crawl to hear you. Tom, what's wrong?"

"I forgive you for everything, Sid. [Groan.] Everything you've ever done to me. When I'm gone—"

"Oh, Tom, you're not dying, are you? Don't, Tom—oh, don't. Maybe—"

"I forgive everyone, Sid. [Groan.] Tell them that, Sid. And Sid, you give my window sash and my one-eyed cat to that new girl who came to town, and tell her—"

But Sid had grabbed his clothes and left. Tom was actually suffering now, since his imagination was working so effectively, and his groans had taken on a completely genuine sound.

Sid rushed downstairs and said:

"Oh, Aunt Polly, come! Tom's dying!"

"Dying!"

"Yes, ma'am. Don't wait—come quick!"

"Nonsense! I don't believe it!"

But she ran upstairs anyway, with Sid and Mary following close behind her. Her face turned pale as well, and her lip began to shake. When she got to the bedside she breathed out heavily:

"You, Tom! Tom, what's wrong with you?"

"Oh, auntie, I'm—"

"What's wrong with you—what is the matter with you, child?"

"Oh, auntie, my sore toe is infected and turning black!"

The elderly woman collapsed into a chair and chuckled softly, then wept quietly, then found herself doing both at the same time. This helped her regain her composure and she said:

"Tom, you really scared me there. Now stop with that foolishness and climb out of here."

The groaning stopped and the pain disappeared from his toe. The boy felt somewhat foolish, and he said:

"Aunt Polly, it felt really embarrassing, and it hurt so much that I completely forgot about my toothache."

"Your tooth, really! What's wrong with your tooth?"

"One of them is loose, and it hurts terribly."

"There, there, now, don't start that groaning again. Open your mouth. Well—your tooth is loose, but you're not going to die from that. Mary, get me a silk thread, and a piece of burning coal from the kitchen."

Tom said:

"Oh, please, Aunt Polly, don't pull it out. It doesn't hurt anymore. I swear it doesn't. Please don't, Aunt Polly. I don't want to stay home from school."

"Oh, you don't, do you? So all this fuss was because you thought you'd get to stay home from school and go fishing? Tom, Tom, I love you so much, and you seem to try every possible way to break my old heart with your terrible behavior." By this time the dental tools were ready. The old woman tied one end of the silk thread securely to Tom's tooth with a loop and fastened the other end to the bedpost. Then she grabbed the piece of burning coal and suddenly thrust it almost into the boy's face. The tooth now hung dangling by the bedpost.

But every hardship comes with its own rewards. As Tom made his way to school after breakfast, every boy he encountered envied him because the missing tooth in his upper row allowed him to spit in a remarkable new way. He attracted quite a crowd of boys fascinated by this display; and another boy who had cut his finger and had been the center of attention and admiration until now suddenly found himself abandoned by his followers and stripped of his fame. He felt dejected, and he declared with a scorn he didn't truly feel that spitting like Tom Sawyer was nothing special; but another boy called out, "Sour grapes!" and he walked away as a fallen hero.

Shortly Tom came across the young outcast of the village, Huckleberry Finn, son of the town drunk. Huckleberry was thoroughly hated and feared by all the mothers in town, because he was lazy and rebellious and crude and bad—and because all their children looked up to him so much, and loved spending time in his forbidden company, and wished they had the courage to be like him. Tom was like all the other respectable boys, in that he was jealous of Huckleberry's flashy outcast status, and was strictly forbidden from playing with him. So he played with him whenever he got the opportunity. Huckleberry was always wearing the discarded clothes of grown men, and they were constantly blooming and flapping with tatters. His hat was a complete wreck with a wide crescent cut out of its brim; his coat, when he had one on, hung almost to his ankles and had the back buttons positioned far down his spine; only one suspender held up his pants; the seat of his trousers sagged low and was empty, the frayed legs dragged in the mud when they weren't rolled up.

Huckleberry came and went whenever he wanted. He slept on doorsteps when the weather was nice and in empty barrels when it rained; he didn't have to attend school or church, or call anyone master or obey anybody; he could go fishing or swimming whenever and wherever he wanted, and stay as long as he felt like it; nobody stopped him from fighting; he could stay up as late as he wanted; he was always the first boy to go barefoot in the spring and the last to put on shoes in the fall; he never had to wash or put on clean clothes; he could curse amazingly well. In short, that boy had everything that makes life wonderful. That's what every stressed, restricted, respectable boy in St. Petersburg thought.

Tom called out to the romantic outcast:

"Hello, Huckleberry!"

"Hello yourself, and see how you like it."

"What's that you got?"

"Dead cat."

"Let me see him, Huck. Wow, he's really stiff. Where did you get him?"

"Bought him from a boy."

"What did you give?"

"I'm offering a blue ticket and a bladder that I picked up from the slaughterhouse."

"Where did you get the blue ticket?"

"Bought it from Ben Rogers two weeks ago for a hoop-stick."

"Tell me—what are dead cats used for, Huck?"

"Good for? Cure warts with."

"No! Is that really true? I know something that's even better."

"I bet you don't. What is it?"

"Why, spunk-water."

"Spunk-water! I wouldn't give a damn for spunk-water."

"You wouldn't, would you? Have you ever tried it?"

"No, I haven't. But Bob Tanner did."

"Who told you that!"

"Well, he told Jeff Thatcher, and Jeff told Johnny Baker, and Johnny told Jim Hollis, and Jim told Ben Rogers, and Ben told a Black boy, and the Black boy told me. There now!"

"Well, what of it? They'll all lie. At least all but the Black man. I don't know him. But I never saw a Black person that wouldn't lie. Shucks! Now you tell me how Bob Tanner did it, Huck."

"He went and stuck his hand into a decaying tree stump filled with rainwater."

"In the daytime?"

"Certainly."

"With his face toward the stump?"

"Yes. At least I think so."

"Did he say anything?"

"I don't think he did. I don't know."

"Aha! Talk about trying to cure warts with stagnant water in such a foolish way as that! Why, that isn't going to do any good. You have to go all by yourself, to the middle of the woods, where you know there's a rotting tree stump filled with water, and just as it's midnight you back up against the stump and stick your hand in and say:

"Barley-corn, barley-corn, injun-meal shorts,
Spunk-water, spunk-water, swallow these warts,"

and then walk away quickly, taking eleven steps with your eyes closed, and then turn around three times and walk home without speaking to anyone. Because if you speak, the charm will be broken.

"Well, that sounds like a good approach, but that's not how Bob Tanner did it."

"No sir, you can bet he didn't, because he's the boy with the most warts in this town; and he wouldn't have a single wart on him if he'd known how to use stump-water. I've removed thousands of warts from my hands that way, Huck. I play with frogs so much that I've always got quite a few warts. Sometimes I remove them with a bean."

"Yes, beans are good. I've tried that."

"Have you? What's your way?"

"You take a bean and split it in half, then cut the wart to draw some blood. Next, you put the blood on one piece of the bean and dig a hole to bury it around midnight at the crossroads during the dark of the moon, then you burn the remaining piece of the bean. You see, the piece with the blood on it will keep pulling and pulling, trying to bring the other piece back to it, and this helps the blood draw out the wart, and pretty soon it falls right off."

"Yes, that's exactly right, Huck—that's it; though when you're burying it, if you say 'Down bean; off wart; come no more to bother me!' it works better. That's how Joe Harper does it, and he's been nearly to Coonville and just about everywhere. But tell me—how do you cure them with dead cats?"

"Why, you take your cat and go to the graveyard around midnight when someone wicked has been buried; and when midnight comes, a devil will appear, or maybe two or three, but you can't see them, you can only hear something like the wind, or maybe hear them talking; and when they're taking that person away, you throw your cat after them and say, 'Devil follow corpse, cat follow devil, warts follow cat, I'm done with you!' That will get rid of any wart."

"That sounds right. Have you ever tried it, Huck?"

"No, but old Mother Hopkins told me."

"Well, I suppose that's true, then. Because they say she's a witch."

"Listen! Tom, I know she's a witch. She put a spell on my father. Dad told me so himself. He was walking along one day, and he saw that she was casting a spell on him, so he picked up a rock, and if she hadn't moved out of the way, he would have hit her. Well, that very same night he rolled off a shed where he was lying drunk, and broke his arm."

"Why, that's terrible. How did he know she was putting a spell on him?"

"Lord, dad can tell easily. Dad says when they keep staring at you steadily, they're putting a spell on you. Especially if they mumble. Because when they mumble they're saying the Lord's Prayer backwards."

"Tell me, Hucky, when are you going to try the cat?"

"Tonight. I think they'll come after old Hoss Williams tonight."

"But they buried him on Saturday. Didn't they find him Saturday night?"

"Why, what are you saying! How could their magic work until midnight?—and then it's Sunday. Devils don't move around much on a Sunday, I don't think."

"I never thought of that. You're right. Can I come with you?"

"Of course—if you're not afraid."

"Afraid! That's not likely. Will you meow?"

"Yes—and you meow back if you get the chance. Last time, you kept me meowing around until old Hays started throwing rocks at me and said 'Damn that cat!' so I threw a brick through his window—but don't tell anyone."

"I won't. I couldn't meow that night, because my aunt was watching me, but I'll meow this time. Tell me—what's that?"

"Nothing but a tick."

"Where did you get him?"

"Out in the woods."

"What will you take for him?"

"I don't know. I don't want to sell him."

"All right. It's a very small tick, anyway."

"Oh, anyone can chase away a tick that doesn't belong to them. I'm happy with it. It's a good enough tick for me."

"Sure, there are plenty of ticks. I could have a thousand of them if I wanted to."

"Well, why don't you? Because you know very well you can't. This is a pretty early tick, I think. It's the first one I've seen this year."

"Listen, Huck—I'll trade you my tooth for him."

"Let's see it."

Tom pulled out a piece of paper and carefully unrolled it. Huckleberry looked at it longingly. The temptation was overwhelming. Finally he said:

"Is it genuine?"

Tom lifted his lip and revealed the empty space.

"Well, all right," said Huckleberry, "it's a deal."

Tom put the tick inside the percussion-cap box that had recently served as the pinchbug's cage, and the boys went their separate ways, each feeling richer than they had before.

When Tom arrived at the small, isolated wooden schoolhouse, he walked in quickly, acting like someone who had hurried there as fast as he could. He hung his hat on a hook and threw himself into his seat with businesslike energy. The teacher, sitting high up in his large cane-bottom armchair like a king on his throne, was dozing, made sleepy by the quiet murmur of students studying. Tom's entrance woke him up.

"Thomas Sawyer!"

Tom knew that whenever someone used his full name, he was in trouble.

"Sir!"

"Come up here. Now, sir, why are you late again, as usual?"

Tom was about to resort to telling a lie when he spotted two long braids of blonde hair cascading down a back that he immediately recognized through the magnetic pull of love; next to that figure was the only empty seat on the girls' side of the schoolhouse. He immediately said:

"I stopped to talk with Huckleberry Finn!"

The teacher's heartbeat stopped, and he stared in shock. The classroom fell silent as studying came to a halt. The students wondered if this reckless boy had completely lost his mind. The teacher said:

"You—you did what?"

"Stopped to talk with Huckleberry Finn."

There was no mistaking the words.

"Thomas Sawyer, this is the most shocking confession I have ever heard. A simple ruler won't be enough punishment for this offense. Take off your jacket."

The teacher's arm worked until it grew weary and the supply of switches was significantly reduced. Then the command came:

"Now, sir, go and sit with the girls! And let this be a warning to you."

The quiet laughter that spread around the room seemed to embarrass the boy, but actually this reaction came more from his reverent admiration of his mysterious crush and the fearful joy he felt at his incredible luck. He sat down at the end of the wooden bench and the girl scooted away from him with a sharp turn of her head. Gentle pushes, winks, and whispered comments moved through the room, but Tom remained motionless, with his arms resting on the long, low desk in front of him, and appeared to focus on his book.

Gradually, attention shifted away from him, and the familiar classroom chatter filled the stale air once again. Soon the boy started sneaking quick looks at the girl. She noticed this, made a face at him, and turned her back to him for about a minute. When she carefully turned around again, a peach was sitting in front of her. She pushed it away. Tom gently placed it back. She pushed it away again, but with less hostility. Tom patiently put it back where it was. Then she left it there. Tom wrote on his slate, "Please take it—I have more." The girl looked at the words but gave no response. Now the boy started drawing something on the slate, covering his work with his left hand. For a while the girl refused to pay attention, but her natural curiosity soon began to show itself through barely noticeable signs. The boy kept working, seemingly unaware. The girl made a kind of uncommitted attempt to look, but the boy didn't reveal that he noticed it. Finally she gave up and hesitantly whispered:

"Let me see it."

Tom partially revealed a gloomy sketch of a house featuring two triangular roof sections and a spiral of smoke rising from the chimney. The girl's attention then became completely absorbed in his artwork, and she forgot about everything else around her. Once he had completed the drawing, she stared at it for a moment before whispering:

"It's nice—make a man."

The artist built a man in the front yard that looked like a derrick. He could have stepped right over the house, but the girl wasn't overly critical; she was happy with the giant figure and whispered:

"It's a beautiful man—now let me come along."

Tom drew an hourglass with a full moon and straw limbs attached to it, and he armed the outstretched fingers with an ominous fan. The girl said:

"It's really wonderful—I wish I could draw."

"It's easy," whispered Tom, "I'll teach you."

"Oh, will you? When?"

"At noon. Do you go home to dinner?"

"I'll stay if you will."

"Good—that's a hit. What's your name?"

"Becky Thatcher. What's yours? Oh, I know. It's Thomas Sawyer."

"That's what they call me when I'm being good. My name is Tom when I behave myself. You'll call me Tom, won't you?"

"Yes."

Now Tom started writing something on the slate, hiding the words from the girl. But she wasn't shy this time. She begged to see. Tom said:

"Oh, it's nothing."

"Yes it is."

"No it isn't. You don't want to see."

"Yes I do, indeed I do. Please let me."

"You'll tell."

"No I won't—absolutely and positively won't."

"You won't tell anyone at all? Ever, for as long as you live?"

"No, I won't ever tell anybody. Now let me."

"Oh, you don't want to see!"

"Now that you're treating me this way, I'll find out." She placed her small hand on his, and a brief struggle followed, with Tom pretending to resist seriously but gradually letting his hand slip until these words were revealed: "I love you."

"Oh, you naughty thing!" And she gave his hand a sharp smack, but her cheeks turned red and she looked pleased all the same.

Right at that moment, the boy felt a slow, deliberate hand gripping his ear and steadily pulling him upward. In this manner, he was carried across the room and placed back in his own seat, while the entire class erupted in a shower of giggles. The teacher then loomed over him for several terrible moments before finally returning to his desk without uttering a single word. Even though

Tom's ear was stinging, his heart was filled with joy.

As the school grew quiet, Tom made a genuine attempt to focus on his studies, but the inner turmoil he felt was overwhelming. He took his turn in the reading class and completely bungled it; then in geography class, he confused lakes with mountains, mountains with rivers, and rivers with continents, creating complete disorder; then in spelling class, he was defeated by a series of simple, elementary words until he ended up at the bottom of the class and had to give up the pewter medal he had proudly displayed for months.

Chapter VII

The harder Tom tried to focus his attention on his book, the more his thoughts drifted away. Finally, with a sigh and a yawn, he gave up completely. It felt like the lunch break would never arrive. The air was completely still. Not even the slightest breeze was moving. It was the most drowsy of drowsy days. The sleepy murmur of the twenty-five students studying had a soothing effect on the spirit, like the enchanting sound of buzzing bees. Far away in the blazing sunlight, Cardiff Hill raised its gentle green slopes through a wavering curtain of heat, colored with the purple hue of distance; a few birds drifted on leisurely wings high above; no other living creature could be seen except for some cows, and they were sleeping. Tom's heart longed to be free, or at least to have something interesting to do to help pass the boring time. His hand drifted into his pocket and his face brightened with a warmth of thankfulness that was like a prayer, though he didn't realize it. Then secretly the percussion-cap box emerged. He let the tick out and placed it on the long flat desk. The little creature probably felt a gratitude that was almost like a prayer too at that moment, but it was too early to celebrate: because when it started to crawl away gratefully, Tom redirected it with a pin and forced it to go in a different direction.

Tom's closest friend sat beside him, experiencing the same suffering Tom had endured, and suddenly he became deeply and gratefully fascinated by this entertainment. This closest friend was Joe Harper. The two boys remained devoted friends throughout the week, yet became fierce rivals on Saturdays. Joe removed a pin from his lapel and started helping to control the prisoner. The amusement became increasingly engaging by the moment. Before long, Tom mentioned that they were getting in each other's way, and neither was gaining the maximum enjoyment from the tick. Therefore, he placed Joe's slate on the desk and drew a line down the center of it from top to bottom.

"Now," he said, "as long as he stays on your side, you can provoke him and I'll leave him be; but if you let him escape and he comes over to my side, you must leave him alone for as long as I can prevent him from crossing back over."

"All right, go ahead; start him up."

The tick got away from Tom for a moment and crossed to the other side. Joe bothered it for a while, and then it escaped and crossed back over again. This switching of sides happened many times. While one boy was bothering the tick with complete focus, the other would watch with equally strong interest, both heads leaning together over the slate, and both minds completely absorbed in nothing else. Finally, luck seemed to favor Joe and stay with him. The tick tried this approach, then that one, and then another direction, becoming as excited and worried as the boys themselves, but again and again just when victory seemed within reach, so to speak, and Tom's fingers were ready to start moving, Joe's pin would skillfully block the tick and maintain control.

Finally, Tom couldn't take it anymore. The temptation was too powerful. So he reached out and helped with his pin. Joe became angry immediately. He said:

"Tom, leave him alone."

"I just want to get him a little worked up, Joe."

"No, sir, it isn't fair; you just leave him alone."

"Damn it, I'm not going to bother him much."

"Leave him alone, I'm telling you."

"I won't!"

"You shall—he's on my side of the line."

"Listen here, Joe Harper, who does that tick belong to?"

"I don't care who he belongs to—he's on my side of the boundary, and you won't lay a hand on him."

"Well, I'll just bet I will, though. He's my tick and I'll do what I darn well please with him, or die!"

A powerful blow struck Tom's shoulders, and an identical one hit Joe's; for two full minutes dust kept flying from both jackets while the entire school delighted in watching. The boys had been so engrossed that they failed to notice the silence that had gradually fallen over the classroom earlier when the teacher came quietly walking down the room and positioned himself above them. He had observed a significant portion of their antics before he added his own contribution to the spectacle.

When school ended at noon, Tom rushed over to Becky Thatcher and whispered in her ear:

"Put on your hat and pretend you're heading home; when you reach the corner, slip away from the others and turn down through the lane to come back. I'll take the other route and fool them the same way."

So one student left with one group of classmates, and the other departed with a different group. Shortly afterward, the two met at the end of the street, and when they arrived at the school they found themselves completely alone. They sat down together with a writing slate in front of them, and Tom handed Becky the pencil and took her hand in his, directing it as they drew another remarkable house. When their enthusiasm for drawing started to fade, they began to chat. Tom felt overwhelmed with happiness. He said:

"Do you love rats?"

"No! I hate them!"

"Well, I do too—living ones. But I'm talking about dead ones, to spin around your head with a string."

"No, I don't really care for rats anyway. What I like is chewing gum."

"Oh, absolutely! I wish I had some right now."

"Do you? I have some. I'll let you chew it for a while, but you have to give it back to me."

That was pleasant, so they took turns chewing it and swung their legs against the bench in pure contentment.

"Have you ever been to a circus?" said Tom.

"Yes, and my dad's going to take me again sometime, if I'm good."

"I've been to the circus three or four times—many times. Church is nothing compared to a circus. There are things happening at a circus all the time. I'm going to be a clown in a circus when I grow up."

"Oh, you are! That will be wonderful. They're so beautiful, all covered in spots."

"Yes, that's true. And they make tons of money—almost a dollar a day, Ben Rogers says. Say, Becky, have you ever been engaged?"

"What's that?"

"Why, engaged to be married."

"No."

"Would you like to?"

"I think so. I don't know. What is it like?"

"Like? Why it's not like anything. You just tell a boy you won't ever have anybody but him, ever ever ever, and then you kiss and that's all. Anybody can do it."

"Kiss? What do you kiss for?"

"Well, you see, that's just—you know, that's what they always do."

"Everybody?"

"Why, yes, everyone who's in love with each other. Do you remember what I wrote on the slate?"

"Ye—yes."

"What was it?"

"I won't tell you."

"Should I tell you?"

"Yes—yes—but some other time."

"No, now."

"No, not now—tomorrow."

"Oh, no, not now. Please, Becky—I'll whisper it, I'll whisper it very quietly."

When Becky hesitated, Tom interpreted her silence as agreement and wrapped his arm around her waist, whispering the story very softly with his mouth close to her ear. Then he added:

"Now you whisper it to me—just the same."

She fought against it for a time, and then said:

"You turn your face away so you can't see, and then I will. But you must never tell anyone—will you, Tom? You won't tell anyone, will you?"

"No, absolutely not, I really won't. Now, Becky."

He turned his face away. She leaned forward hesitantly until her breath touched his hair and whispered, "I—love—you!"

Then she jumped up and ran in circles around the desks and benches, with Tom chasing after her, and finally took shelter in a corner with her little white apron covering her face. Tom put his arms around her neck and begged:

"Now, Becky, it's all finished—everything's over except for the kiss. Don't be scared of that—it's really nothing at all. Please, Becky." And he pulled at her apron and her hands.

Eventually she gave up and let her hands fall to her sides; her face, flushed from the struggle, lifted up in surrender. Tom kissed her red lips and said:

"Now it's all finished, Becky. And from now on, you know, you're never going to love anyone but me, and you're never going to marry anyone but me, not ever and forever. Will you promise?"

"No, I'll never love anyone but you, Tom, and I'll never marry anyone but you—and you're not allowed to ever marry anyone but me, either."

"Absolutely. Of course. That's part of it. And whenever we're coming to school or going home, you have to walk with me when nobody's watching—and you pick me and I pick you at parties, because that's what you do when you're engaged."

"It's so nice. I never heard of it before."

"Oh, it's so much fun! Why, Amy Lawrence and I—"

The wide eyes revealed to Tom that he had made a mistake, and he halted, bewildered.

"Oh, Tom! Then I'm not the first person you've ever been engaged to!"

The child started to cry. Tom said:

"Oh, don't cry, Becky, I don't care about her anymore."

"Yes, you do, Tom—you know you do."

Tom attempted to wrap his arm around her neck, but she shoved him away and turned her face toward the wall, continuing to cry. Tom made another attempt, speaking gentle words, but was rejected once more. His pride then flared up, and he walked away and went outside. He lingered there, restless and anxious, for some time, occasionally glancing at the door, hoping she would change her mind and come looking for him. But she didn't. Then he started to feel terrible and worried that he might be wrong. It was difficult for him to make another attempt at reconciliation, but he gathered his courage and went back inside. She was still standing in the corner, weeping, with her face turned to the wall. Tom felt a pang of guilt. He approached her and stood there for a moment, uncertain about how to proceed. Then he said hesitantly:

"Becky, I—I don't care for anybody but you."

No reply—but sobs.

"Becky"—pleadingly. "Becky, won't you say something?"

More sobs.

Tom pulled out his most prized possession, a brass knob from the top of a fireplace iron, and held it out for her to see, saying:

"Please, Becky, won't you take it?"

She knocked it to the floor. Then Tom walked out of the house and over the hills and far away, never to return to school that day. Soon Becky started to get suspicious. She ran to the door; he was nowhere to be seen; she rushed around to the playground; he wasn't there either. Then she called out:

"Tom! Come back, Tom!"

She listened carefully, but no response came. Silence and loneliness were her only companions. So she sat down to cry once more and scold herself; and by this time the students began to return, and she had to conceal her sorrows and quiet her broken heart and bear the burden of a long, gloomy, painful afternoon, with no one among the unfamiliar faces around her to share her troubles with.

Chapter VIII

Tom weaved back and forth through the narrow streets until he was far away from the path where other students would be heading home, and then he settled into a gloomy walk. He crossed a small stream two or three times, following a common childhood belief that crossing water would throw off anyone who might be chasing him. Thirty minutes later he was vanishing behind the Douglas house on top of Cardiff Hill, and the schoolhouse was barely visible far away in the valley below him. He went into a thick forest, found his way without following any trail to the center of it, and sat down on a moss-covered spot beneath a wide-spreading oak tree. There wasn't even a gentle breeze moving; the oppressive midday heat had silenced even the birds' songs; nature seemed to be in a deep sleep that was interrupted by no sound except the occasional distant tapping of a woodpecker, and this only made the overwhelming quiet and feeling of isolation seem even deeper. The boy's spirit was filled with sadness; his emotions perfectly matched his surroundings. He sat for a long time with his elbows resting on his knees and his chin cupped in his hands, thinking deeply. It seemed to him that life was nothing but trouble, at best, and he more than half wished he could be like Jimmy Hodges, who had recently died; it must be very peaceful, he thought, to lie there sleeping and dreaming forever and ever, with the wind whispering through the trees and gently touching the grass and flowers over the grave, and nothing to worry about or feel sad about, ever again. If only he had a perfect Sunday school attendance record he would be willing to go, and be finished with everything. Now about this girl. What had he done wrong? Nothing. He had meant well and tried his best, and been treated like a dog—like a worthless dog. She would feel sorry someday—maybe when it was too late. Oh, if he could only die temporarily!

But the flexible heart of youth cannot be squeezed into one rigid form for very long. Tom soon began to drift unconsciously back into the worries of everyday life again. What if he turned around now and vanished without a trace? What if he left—traveling far, far away to mysterious lands across the oceans—and never returned! How would she feel then! The thought of becoming a clown came back to him now, only to fill him with revulsion. For silliness and humor and polka-dotted costumes were insulting when they forced themselves upon a soul that had been lifted into the mysterious noble world of romance. No, he would become a soldier and return after many years, battle-scarred and famous. No—even better, he would join the Indians and hunt buffalo and go to war in the mountain ranges and the endless vast plains of the Far West, and sometime in the future return as a great chief, covered with feathers, frightening with war paint, and stride into Sunday school on some sleepy summer morning with a spine-chilling war cry, and burn the eyes of all his friends with unstoppable jealousy. But no, there was something even more spectacular than this. He would become a pirate! That was it! Now his future stretched out clearly before him, shining with incredible magnificence. How his name would echo throughout the world and make people tremble! How magnificently he would sail across the rolling seas in his long, sleek, black-hulled ship, the Spirit of the Storm, with his terrifying flag flying at the front! And at the peak of his glory, how he would suddenly appear at the old village and march into church, tanned and weathered, wearing his black velvet jacket and pants, his tall leather boots, his bright red sash, his belt loaded with pistols, his blood-stained sword at his side, his wide-brimmed hat with flowing feathers, his black flag displayed with the skull and crossbones on it, and listen with growing excitement to the whispers, "It's Tom Sawyer the Pirate!—the Black Avenger of the Spanish Main!"

Yes, it was decided; his future was set. He would run away from home and begin this new life. He would leave the very next morning. So he needed to start preparing right away. He would gather all his belongings together. He walked over to a decaying log nearby and started digging underneath one end of it with his Barlow knife. Soon he hit wood that made a hollow sound. He placed his hand on that spot and spoke this spell with great drama:

"What hasn't come here, come! What's here, stay here!"

Then he brushed away the dirt and revealed a pine shingle underneath. He lifted it up and uncovered a neat little treasure box with a bottom and sides made of shingles. Inside it was a marble. Tom was absolutely amazed! He scratched his head, looking completely puzzled, and said:

"Well, that beats anything!"

Then he threw the marble away in frustration and stood there thinking. The reality was that one of his superstitions had failed him here, something that he and all his friends had always believed was foolproof. If you buried a marble while performing certain required rituals, left it undisturbed for two weeks, and then reopened the spot using the incantation he had just tried, you would discover that all the marbles you had ever lost had somehow gathered themselves together in that place, regardless of how far apart they had been scattered. But now, this method had clearly and undeniably failed. Tom's entire belief system was shaken to its core. He had heard countless stories of this technique working but had never heard of it failing before. It didn't cross his mind that he had attempted this several times previously but could never locate the burial spots afterward. He pondered the situation for a while and eventually concluded that some witch had meddled and broken the spell. He decided he would confirm this theory, so he looked around until he discovered a small patch of sand with a tiny funnel-shaped hollow in it. He lay down on the ground and placed his mouth near this hollow and called out—

"Doodle-bug, doodle-bug, tell me what I want to know! Doodle-bug, doodle-bug, tell me what I want to know!"

The sand started to shift, and soon a tiny black insect emerged briefly before quickly disappearing back underneath in alarm.

"He doesn't dare tell! So it was a witch who did it. I just knew it."

He understood completely how pointless it would be to fight against witches, so he abandoned his efforts in defeat. However, it crossed his mind that he might as well retrieve the marble he had just discarded, so he went and conducted a thorough search for it. Yet he was unable to locate it. He then returned to his treasure location and positioned himself precisely as he had been standing when he threw the marble away; next he pulled another marble from his pocket and threw it in the same manner, saying:

"Brother, go find your brother!"

He watched where it landed and walked over to check. But it must have fallen short or gone too far, so he tried two more times. The final attempt worked. The two marbles ended up within a foot of each other.

At that moment, the faint sound of a toy tin trumpet drifted through the green corridors of the forest. Tom threw off his jacket and pants, converted a suspender into a belt, brushed away some undergrowth from behind the decaying log, revealing a crude bow and arrow, a wooden sword, and a tin trumpet. Within moments he had grabbed these items and sprinted away barefoot, his shirt billowing behind him. Soon he stopped beneath a massive elm tree, blew a responding blast on his trumpet, and then began to move stealthily on his toes, scanning cautiously in all directions. He spoke quietly to an imaginary group:

"Wait, my loyal men! Stay hidden until I give the signal."

Now Joe Harper appeared, dressed just as lightly and carrying just as many elaborate weapons as Tom. Tom called out:

"Stop! Who enters Sherwood Forest without my permission?"

"Guy of Guisborne doesn't need anyone's permission to pass. Who are you that—that—"

"Dares to speak that way," said Tom, giving him a cue—since they were reciting "from the book," relying on what they had memorized.

"Who are you to dare speak like that?"

"I certainly am! I'm Robin Hood, as your worthless body will soon discover."

"So you're really that famous outlaw? I'll gladly fight you for control of these forest paths. Let's go!"

They grabbed their wooden swords, dropped their other gear on the ground, took up proper fencing positions with their feet positioned correctly, and started a serious, deliberate fight using the "two up and two down" technique. After a moment, Tom said:

"Now, if you've got the hang of it, go at it with energy!"

So they "went at it with energy," breathing hard and sweating from the effort. Soon Tom called out:

"Fall! fall! Why don't you fall?"

"I won't! Why don't you fall down yourself? You're losing badly."

"Why, that's nothing at all. I can't fall down; that's not how it happens in the book. The book says, 'Then with one back-handed stroke he slew poor Guy of Guisborne.' You're supposed to turn around and let me hit you in the back."

There was no way to avoid the authorities, so Joe turned around, took the blow, and collapsed.

"Now," said Joe, standing up, "you have to let me kill you. That's only fair."

"Why, I can't do that, it's not in the book."

"Well, it's really mean—that's all."

"Well, listen Joe, you can be Friar Tuck or Much the miller's son, and hit me with a quarterstaff; or I'll be the Sheriff of

Nottingham and you be Robin Hood for a while and kill me."

This arrangement worked well, and the boys carried out these adventures. Then Tom took on the role of Robin Hood once more, and the treacherous nun was permitted to let him slowly lose his strength through his untreated wound. Finally, Joe, playing the part of an entire tribe of mourning outlaws, sorrowfully pulled him forward, placed his bow in his weakened hands, and Tom declared, "Where this arrow lands, there bury poor Robin Hood beneath the greenwood tree." He then shot the arrow and collapsed backward, appearing ready to die, but he landed on a stinging nettle and jumped up far too cheerfully for someone who was supposed to be dead.

The boys got dressed, hid their equipment, and left feeling sad that there were no more outlaws, wondering what modern civilization could possibly offer to make up for what they had lost. They said they would rather spend a year as outlaws in Sherwood Forest than be President of the United States for life.

Chapter IX

At nine-thirty that night, Tom and Sid were sent to bed as usual. They said their prayers, and Sid quickly fell asleep. Tom lay awake and waited, filled with restless impatience. When he thought it must be nearly dawn, he heard the clock strike ten! This filled him with despair. He wanted to toss and turn as his nerves demanded, but he was afraid he might wake Sid. So he lay perfectly still and stared up into the darkness. Everything was eerily quiet. Gradually, out of the silence, small, barely noticeable sounds began to stand out. The ticking of the clock started to draw attention to itself. Old wooden beams began to crack mysteriously. The stairs creaked softly. Clearly, spirits were moving about. A steady, muffled snoring came from Aunt Polly's bedroom. And then the annoying chirping of a cricket that no human cleverness could find began. Next, the horrible ticking of a death-watch beetle in the wall near the head of his bed made Tom shiver—it meant that someone's days were numbered. Then the howling of a distant dog rose into the night air and was answered by a fainter howl from an even more remote distance. Tom was in agony. Finally, he became convinced that time had stopped and eternity had begun; he started to drift off despite himself; the clock struck eleven, but he didn't hear it. And then there came, mixing with his half-formed dreams, a most sorrowful caterwauling. The opening of a nearby window disturbed him. A shout of "Get out of here, you devil!" and the crash of an empty bottle against the back of his aunt's woodshed brought him fully awake, and just one minute later he was dressed and out the window, crawling along the roof of the addition on his hands and knees. He meowed cautiously once or twice as he moved; then he jumped to the roof of the woodshed and from there to the ground. Huckleberry Finn was waiting there with his dead cat. The boys moved away and vanished into the darkness. After half an hour, they were walking through the tall grass of the graveyard.

It was an old-style Western graveyard. The cemetery sat on a hill, roughly a mile and a half away from the village. A rickety wooden fence surrounded it, tilting inward in some spots and outward in others, never standing completely straight anywhere. Thick grass and weeds had taken over the entire burial ground. All the older graves had collapsed inward, and there wasn't a single proper tombstone anywhere on the property; curved wooden boards, eaten through by worms, wobbled unsteadily over the graves, searching for something to lean against but finding no support. "Sacred to the memory of" someone or other had once been painted on these boards, but the words could no longer be made out on most of them, even if there had been enough light to see.

A gentle breeze whispered through the trees, and Tom worried it might be the ghosts of the dead, upset about being bothered. The boys spoke very little, and only in whispers, because the late hour and the location and the overwhelming seriousness and quiet weighed heavily on their minds. They discovered the fresh mound of dirt they had been looking for, and settled themselves under the shelter of three large elm trees that stood clustered together just a few feet from the grave.

Then they waited quietly for what felt like a very long time. The distant call of an owl was the only sound that broke the complete silence. Tom's thoughts became overwhelming. He needed to start a conversation. So he whispered:

"Hucky, do you think dead people like us being here?"

Huckleberry whispered:

"I wish I knew. It feels really serious, doesn't it?"

"I bet it is."

There was a long pause while the boys thought this over silently. Then Tom whispered:

"Tell me, Hucky—do you think Hoss Williams can hear us talking?"

"Of course he does. At least his spirit does."

Tom, after a pause:

"I wish I had said Mister Williams. But I never meant any harm. Everybody calls him Hoss."

"A person can't be too careful about how they talk about these dead people, Tom."

This put a damper on things, and the conversation died out once more.

Tom suddenly grabbed his friend's arm and said:

"Sh!"

“What’s wrong, Tom?” The two held each other close, their hearts pounding.

“Shh! There it is again! Didn’t you hear it?”

“I—”

“There! Now you hear it.”

“Lord, Tom, they’re coming! They’re coming, for sure. What are we going to do?”

“I don’t know. Do you think they’ll see us?”

“Oh, Tom, they can see in the dark, just like cats. I wish I hadn’t come.”

“Oh, don’t be afraid. I don’t think they’ll bother us. We aren’t doing anything wrong. If we stay completely still, maybe they won’t notice us at all.”

“I’ll try to, Tom, but Lord, I’m shaking all over.”

“Listen!”

The boys leaned their heads close together and barely dared to breathe. A quiet murmur of voices drifted up from the distant end of the graveyard.

“Look! See there!” Tom whispered. “What is it?”

“It’s devil-fire. Oh, Tom, this is awful.”

Some shadowy figures came closer through the darkness, carrying an old-style tin lantern that scattered countless tiny spots of light across the ground. Soon Huckleberry whispered with a shiver:

“Those are definitely devils. Three of them! Oh Lord, Tom, we’re done for! Can you pray?”

“I’ll try, but don’t be afraid. They’re not going to hurt us. ‘Now I lay me down to sleep, I—’”

“Sh!”

“What is it, Huck?”

“They’re humans! One of them is, anyway. One of them has old Muff Potter’s voice.”

“No—that’s not true, is it?”

"I bet I know what's going on. Don't move or make a sound. He's not alert enough to spot us. Probably drunk as always—that worthless old fool!"

"Alright, I'll stay quiet. Now they're stuck. They can't find it. Here they come again. Now they're getting close. Cold again. Getting close again. Very close! They're pointing in the right direction this time. Hey, Huck, I recognize another one of those voices; it's Injun Joe."

"That's right—that murderous half-breed! I'd rather they were devils by a long shot. What could they be up to?"

The whisper faded away completely now, as the three men had reached the grave and were standing just a few feet from where the boys were hiding.

"Here it is," said the third voice, and whoever was speaking lifted the lantern up, revealing the face of young Doctor Robinson.

Potter and Injun Joe were carrying a wheelbarrow loaded with rope and a pair of shovels. They set down their burden and started digging up the grave. The doctor placed the lantern at the head of the burial site and walked over to sit with his back resting against one of the elm trees. He was positioned so near that the boys could have reached out and touched him.

"Hurry, men!" he said, in a low voice; "the moon might come out at any moment."

They grumbled a reply and continued digging. For a while, the only sound was the scraping noise of shovels dumping their loads of dirt and gravel. The work was incredibly repetitive. Eventually, a shovel hit the coffin with a hollow, wooden thud, and within a minute or two, the men had pulled it up onto the ground. They forced off the lid with their shovels, removed the body, and carelessly dropped it on the ground. The moon emerged from behind the clouds and revealed the pale face. The wheelbarrow was prepared and the corpse was placed on it, covered with a blanket, and tied down with rope. Potter pulled out a large spring-knife and cut off the hanging end of the rope and then said:

"Now the damn thing's ready, Doctor, and you'll just hand over another five dollars, or it stays right here."

"That's the talk!" said Injun Joe.

"Listen, what's the meaning of this?" the doctor said. "You demanded your payment upfront, and I've already paid you."

"Yes, and you did more than that," said Injun Joe, approaching the doctor, who was now standing. "Five years ago you drove me away from your father's kitchen one night, when I came to ask for something to eat, and you said I wasn't there for any good; and when I swore I'd get even with you if it took a hundred years, your father had me jailed for being a vagrant. Did you think I'd forget? The Indian blood isn't in me for nothing. And now I've got you, and you have to settle up, you know!"

He was threatening the doctor by this point, shaking his fist right in the man's face. The doctor suddenly lashed out and knocked the thug to the ground. Potter let his knife fall and cried out:

"Stop right there! Don't you dare hit my partner!" and the next moment he had grabbed hold of the doctor and the two men were fighting with all their strength, stomping on the grass and digging up the ground with their heels. Injun Joe jumped to his feet, his eyes burning with rage, grabbed Potter's knife, and began moving like a cat, crouched low, circling around and around the two fighting men, looking for his chance to strike. Suddenly the doctor broke free, grabbed the heavy wooden headstone from Williams' grave and knocked Potter to the ground with it—and at that exact moment the half-breed saw his opportunity and plunged the knife all the way to its handle into the young man's chest. The doctor staggered and collapsed partially on top of Potter, covering him with his blood, and at that same instant the clouds covered the horrible scene and the two terrified boys ran away as fast as they could into the darkness.

Right then, when the moon came out again, Injun Joe was standing over the two bodies, staring down at them. The doctor mumbled something unclear, let out a long breath or two, and then went silent. The half-breed muttered:

"That score is settled—damn you."

Then he robbed the body. After that, he placed the deadly knife in Potter's open right hand and sat down on the broken coffin. Three, four, five minutes went by, and then Potter started to move and groan. His hand gripped the knife; he lifted it up, looked at it, and dropped it with a shudder. Then he sat up, pushing the body away from him, and stared at it, and then looked around him in confusion. His eyes met Joe's.

"Lord, how is this, Joe?" he said.

"It's a dirty business," said Joe, without moving. "What did you do it for?"

"I! I never did it!"

"Listen! That kind of talk won't work."

Potter trembled and turned pale.

"I thought I had gotten sober. I had no business drinking tonight. But it's still in my head—worse than when we started here. I'm all confused; I can barely remember anything about it. Tell me, Joe—honestly now, old friend—did I do it? Joe, I never intended to—upon my soul and honor, I never intended to, Joe. Tell me how it happened, Joe. Oh, it's terrible—and him so young and promising."

"Why, you two were fighting, and he hit you with the headboard and you fell down flat; and then you got up, all wobbly and staggering, and grabbed the knife and stabbed it into him, just as he gave you another terrible blow—and here you've been lying, as dead as a doornail until now."

"Oh, I didn't know what I was doing. I wish I may die this minute if I did. It was all because of the whiskey and the excitement, I think. I never used a weapon in my life before, Joe.

I've fought, but never with weapons. They'll all say that. Joe, don't tell! Say you won't tell, Joe—that's a good fellow. I always liked you, Joe, and stood up for you, too. Don't you remember? You won't tell, will you, Joe?" And the poor creature dropped on his knees before the emotionless murderer, and clasped his pleading hands.

"No, you've always been honest and straightforward with me, Muff Potter, and I won't turn my back on you. There, now, that's as fair as anyone can say."

"Oh, Joe, you're an angel. I'll bless you for this for the rest of my life." And Potter started to cry.

"Come on, that's enough of that. This isn't the time for crying. You go that way and I'll go this way. Move now, and don't leave any tracks behind you."

Potter began with a quick trot that soon turned into a full run. The half-breed remained standing there, watching him go. He muttered:

"If he's as dazed from the blow and confused by the rum as he appeared to be, he won't think about the knife until he's gone so far that he'll be too scared to come back alone to get it from such a place—coward!"

Two or three minutes later, the murdered man, the covered body, the coffin without a lid, and the open grave had no one watching them except the moon. The silence was complete once more.

Chapter X

The two boys continued flying forward toward the village, struck silent by their terror. They kept looking back over their shoulders with growing anxiety, as though something might be chasing them. Every tree stump that appeared in their path looked like a person and a threat, making their hearts skip a beat; and as they rushed past the scattered houses on the outskirts of the village, the barking of the awakened guard dogs seemed to make them run even faster.

"If we can just make it to the old tannery before we collapse!" Tom whispered in short gasps between breaths. "I can't take much more of this."

Huckleberry's heavy breathing was his only response, and the boys focused their eyes on what they desperately hoped to reach and threw themselves into their effort to get there. They steadily closed the distance, and finally, side by side, they rushed through the open doorway and collapsed thankfully and worn out in the protective darkness beyond. Gradually their heartbeats returned to normal, and Tom whispered:

"Huckleberry, what do you think will come of this?"

"If Doctor Robinson dies, I think someone will end up getting hanged for it."

"Do you though?"

"Why, I know it, Tom."

Tom thought for a moment, then he said:

"Who's going to tell? Us?"

"What are you talking about? Suppose something happened and Injun Joe didn't hang? Why, he'd kill us some time or other, just as dead sure as we're lying here."

"That's exactly what I was thinking, Huck."

"If anyone talks, let Muff Potter be the one to do it, if he's foolish enough. He's usually drunk enough."

Tom remained silent and continued thinking. After a moment, he whispered:

"Huck, Muff Potter doesn't know it. How can he tell?"

"Why doesn't he know it?"

"Because he had just received that blow when Injun Joe did it. Do you think he could see anything? Do you think he knew anything?"

"By golly, that's right, Tom!"

"And besides, look here—maybe that blow killed him!"

"No, that's not likely, Tom. He had alcohol in him; I could see that; and besides, he always does. Well, when dad's drunk, you could take and hit him over the head with a church and you couldn't affect him. He says so himself. So it's the same with Muff Potter, of course. But if a man was completely sober, I think maybe that blow might knock him out; I don't know."

After another thoughtful pause, Tom said:

"Hucky, are you sure you can keep quiet?"

"Tom, we have to keep quiet. You know that. That Indian devil wouldn't think twice about drowning us like a couple of cats if we were to say anything about this and they didn't hang him. Now, listen here, Tom, let's make a promise to each other—that's what we need to do—swear to keep quiet."

"I agree. It's the best thing. Would you just hold hands and swear that we—"

"Oh no, that won't work for this. That's fine for small, worthless ordinary things—especially with girls, because they'll turn against you anyway and tell everyone if they get upset—but there should be something written about a big thing like this. And blood."

Tom's entire being embraced this idea. It was profound, dark, and terrible; the time, the situation, and the environment all matched it perfectly. He picked up a clean piece of pine wood that was lying in the moonlight, pulled a small piece of red chalk from his pocket, positioned his work in the moonlight, and carefully scratched out these words, emphasizing each downward stroke by pressing his tongue between his teeth and easing the pressure on the upward strokes.

"Huck Finn and Tom Sawyer swear they will keep quiet about this and they wish they may drop down dead in their tracks if they ever tell and rot."

Huckleberry was amazed by how easily Tom could write and how impressive his words sounded. He immediately pulled a pin from his jacket and was about to poke his skin, but Tom stopped him:

"Wait! Don't do that. A pin is made of brass. It could have verdigris on it."

"What's verdigris?"

"It's poison. That's what it is. You just swallow some of it once—you'll see."

Tom unwound the thread from one of his needles, and each boy pricked the tip of his thumb and squeezed out a drop of blood. After many squeezes, Tom finally managed to sign his initials, using the pad of his little finger as a pen. He then showed Huckleberry how to make an H and an F, and their oath was complete. They buried the wooden shingle close to the wall with some somber ceremonies and magical words, and the bonds that kept their tongues silent were considered locked tight with the key thrown away.

A figure quietly slipped through an opening at the far end of the crumbling building, but they didn't see it.

"Tom," Huckleberry whispered, "does this prevent us from ever telling anyone—forever?"

"Of course it does. It doesn't make any difference what happens, we have to keep quiet. We'd drop down dead—don't you know that?"

"Yes, I think that's right."

They kept whispering quietly for a while. Soon a dog began a long, mournful howl just outside—less than ten feet away from them. The boys suddenly grabbed each other, terrified.

"Which one of us is he talking about?" Huckleberry gasped.

"I don't know—look through the crack. Quick!"

"No, you, Tom!"

"I can't—I can't do it, Huck!"

"Please, Tom. There it is again!"

"Oh, thank God!" Tom whispered. "I recognize his voice. It's Bull Harbison." *

[* If Mr. Harbison owned a slave named Bull, Tom would have referred to him as "Harbison's Bull," but a son or a dog with that name would be called "Bull Harbison."]

"Oh, that's good—I tell you, Tom, I was scared to death; I would have bet anything it was a stray dog."

The dog howled again. The boys' hearts sank once more.

"Oh my! That's not Bull Harbison!" whispered Huckleberry. "Come on, Tom!"

Tom, trembling with fear, gave in and pressed his eye to the crack. His whisper was barely audible when he said:

"Oh, Huck, it's a stray dog!"

"Quick, Tom, quick! Who does he mean?"

"Huck, he must mean both of us—we're right here together."

"Oh, Tom, I think we're done for. I think there's no mistake about where I'll end up. I've been so wicked."

"Darn it! This is what happens when you skip school and do everything you're told not to do. I could have been good, like Sid, if I had tried—but no, I wouldn't, of course. But if I ever get out of this mess, I swear I'll throw myself into Sunday school!" And Tom began to sniffle a little.

"You're terrible!" and Huckleberry started to sniffle as well. "Damn it, Tom Sawyer, you're nothing compared to how bad I am. Oh, God, God, God, I wish I had even half your opportunities."

Tom stopped abruptly and whispered:

"Look, Hucky, look! He's got his back to us!"

Hucky looked, with joy in his heart.

"Well, he certainly has! Did he before?"

"Yes, he did. But I, like an idiot, never considered it. Oh, this is great, you know. Now who could he be talking about?"

The howling stopped. Tom listened carefully.

"Sh! What's that?" he whispered.

"It sounds like—like pigs grunting. No—it's someone snoring, Tom."

"That's it! Where exactly is it, Huck?"

"I believe it's down at the other end. It sounds like it, anyway. Dad used to sleep there sometimes, along with the hogs, but goodness, he just lifts things when he snores. Besides, I think he isn't ever coming back to this town anymore."

The spirit of adventure awakened in the boys' hearts once again.

"Hucky, do you dare to go if I lead?"

"I really don't want to, Tom. What if it's Injun Joe!"

Tom felt afraid. But soon the temptation grew strong again and the boys decided to try, agreeing that they would run away if the snoring stopped. So they crept down quietly on their toes, one following behind the other. When they got within five steps of the person snoring, Tom stepped on a stick, and it snapped with a sharp crack. The man groaned, twisted a little, and his face appeared in the moonlight. It was Muff Potter. The boys' hearts stopped, and so did their hopes, when the man moved, but their fears disappeared now. They tiptoed out through the broken wooden boards and stopped a short distance away to say a final word to each other. That long, mournful howl rose into the night air again! They turned and saw the strange dog standing just a few feet from where Potter was lying, facing Potter with his nose pointed toward the sky.

"Oh my goodness, it's him!" both boys exclaimed at the same time.

"Listen, Tom—people say a stray dog came howling around Johnny Miller's house around midnight about two weeks ago, and a whippoorwill flew in and perched on the banister and sang that very same evening, but nobody there has died yet."

"Well, I know that. And suppose there isn't. Didn't Gracie Miller fall in the kitchen fire and burn herself terribly the very next Saturday?"

"Yes, but she isn't dead. And what's more, she's getting better, too."

"All right, you wait and see. She's a goner, just as dead sure as Muff Potter's a goner. That's what the Black folks say, and they know all about these kind of things, Huck."

Then they went their separate ways, each lost in thought. When Tom quietly climbed through his bedroom window, the night was nearly over. He took off his clothes with extreme care and drifted off to sleep, pleased with himself that no one knew about his adventure. He had no idea that Sid, who was softly snoring, was actually awake and had been for an hour.

When Tom woke up, Sid had already gotten dressed and left. The light coming through the window looked late, and there was something in the air that felt like the day was well underway. This startled him. Why hadn't anyone called him or bothered him until he got up, like they usually did? This thought filled him with a sense of dread. Within five minutes he had gotten dressed and made his way downstairs, feeling sore and sleepy. The family was still sitting at the table, but they had already finished eating breakfast. No one scolded him, but everyone avoided looking at him; there was a quiet, serious atmosphere that sent a chill through the guilty boy's heart. He sat down and tried to act cheerful, but it was difficult; his efforts didn't bring any smiles or responses from anyone, so he fell silent and let his spirits sink completely.

After breakfast, his aunt pulled him aside, and Tom's spirits almost lifted with the hope that he was about to receive a beating; however, that wasn't the case. His aunt cried over him and asked how he could go and shatter her elderly heart like this; she finally told him to continue on his path, destroy himself, and send her gray hair to the grave in sorrow, since there was no point in her trying anymore. This felt worse than a thousand beatings, and Tom's heart now ached more than his body ever had. He wept, begged for forgiveness, promised repeatedly to change his ways, and then was sent away, knowing that he had only earned partial forgiveness and gained only weak trust.

He walked away feeling too wretched to even want revenge against Sid; Sid's quick escape through the back gate wasn't needed. He trudged to school feeling gloomy and dejected, and endured his beating alongside Joe Harper for skipping school the previous day, carrying himself like someone whose heart was consumed with much deeper sorrows and completely numb to minor troubles. Then he made his way to his seat, placed his elbows on his desk with his chin resting in his hands, and gazed at the wall with the blank stare of someone whose suffering had reached its breaking point and couldn't get any worse. His elbow was pushing against something hard. After a while, he slowly and sadly shifted his position and picked up the object with a sigh. It was wrapped in paper. He unwrapped it. A long, drawn-out, enormous sigh escaped him, and his heart shattered. It was his brass andiron knob!

This final straw broke the camel's back.

Chapter XI

Around noon, the entire village was suddenly shocked by the horrifying news. There was no need for the telegraph, which hadn't even been invented yet; the story spread from person to person, from one group to another, from house to house, almost as fast as a telegraph could carry it. Naturally, the schoolmaster canceled classes for that afternoon; the townspeople would have found it very strange if he hadn't.

A bloody knife had been discovered near the murdered man, and someone had identified it as belonging to Muff Potter—or so the story went. People were also saying that a late-night citizen had stumbled upon Potter washing himself in the creek around one or two in the morning, and that Potter had immediately slipped away—suspicious behavior, particularly the washing, which wasn't typical for Potter. Word was that the town had been searched thoroughly for this "murderer" (the public doesn't waste time when it comes to examining evidence and reaching a conclusion), but he was nowhere to be found. Riders had set out on all the roads in every direction, and the Sheriff "felt certain" that Potter would be caught before nightfall.

The entire town was moving toward the cemetery. Tom's sadness disappeared and he joined the crowd, not because he wouldn't have preferred to go anywhere else a thousand times over, but because a terrible, mysterious pull drew him forward. When he reached the awful place, he squeezed his small body through the crowd and witnessed the grim scene. It felt like forever since he had been there before. Someone pinched his arm. He turned around, and his eyes met Huckleberry's. Both immediately looked away and wondered if anyone had noticed anything in the look they shared. But everyone was talking and focused on the gruesome sight in front of them.

"Poor guy!" "Poor young man!" "This should teach grave robbers a lesson!" "Muff Potter will be executed for this if they catch him!" This was the general tone of the comments; and the minister said, "It was divine judgment; God's hand is at work here."

Now Tom trembled from head to toe, as his gaze landed on Injun Joe's emotionless face. Just then the crowd started to push and jostle, with voices crying out, "It's him! It's him! He's coming himself!"

"Who? Who?" came from twenty voices.

"Muff Potter!"

"Hey, he's stopped!—Watch out, he's turning! Don't let him get away!"

People sitting in the tree branches above Tom's head said he wasn't attempting to escape—he simply appeared uncertain and confused.

"What incredible nerve!" said someone watching; "he probably wanted to come back and quietly admire what he'd done—didn't think anyone else would be around."

The crowd scattered, and the Sheriff pushed through, making a show of leading Potter by the arm. The poor man's face was drawn and exhausted, and his eyes revealed the terror that gripped him. When he stood before the dead man, he trembled uncontrollably, and he covered his face with his hands and broke into tears.

"I didn't do it, friends," he sobbed; "I swear on my word and honor I never did it."

"Who's accused you?" shouted a voice.

This shot seemed to hit its mark. Potter raised his face and looked around with a pitiful sense of despair in his eyes. He spotted Injun Joe and cried out:

"Oh, Injun Joe, you promised me you'd never—"

"Is that your knife?" and the Sheriff thrust it in front of him.

Potter would have collapsed if they hadn't caught him and helped him down to the ground. Then he said:

"Something told me that if I didn't come back and get—" He shuddered; then waved his weak hand with a defeated gesture and said, "Tell them, Joe, tell them—it's no use anymore."

Then Huckleberry and Tom stood speechless and staring, listening to the cold-hearted liar deliver his calm statement, expecting at any moment that the clear sky would send down God's lightning upon his head, and wondering why the strike was taking so long. And when he had finished speaking and still stood there alive and unharmed, their wavering urge to break their promise and save the poor wrongly accused prisoner's life faded and disappeared, because clearly this villain had made a deal with Satan and it would be dangerous to interfere with the property of such a powerful force.

"Why didn't you leave? What did you want to come here for?" someone asked.

"I couldn't help it—I couldn't help it," Potter groaned. "I wanted to run away, but I couldn't manage to go anywhere except here." And he started sobbing again.

Injun Joe calmly repeated his statement a few minutes later during the inquest, while under oath. The boys watched, and when they saw that lightning still didn't strike him down, they became even more convinced that Joe had made a deal with the devil. He had now become the most frighteningly fascinating person they had ever seen, and they couldn't tear their captivated eyes away from his face.

They secretly decided to keep watch over him at night whenever they got the chance, hoping to catch a glimpse of his terrifying master.

Injun Joe helped lift the murdered man's body and load it into a wagon to be taken away. Word spread through the horrified crowd that the wound had started bleeding slightly! The boys believed this fortunate sign would point suspicion toward the real killer, but they were let down when several townspeople commented:

"It was within three feet of Muff Potter when it happened."

Tom's frightening secret and his guilty conscience kept him awake for about a week after this incident; and one morning at breakfast Sid said:

"Tom, you toss and turn and talk in your sleep so much that you keep me awake half the night."

Tom turned pale and looked down.

"It's a bad sign," said Aunt Polly, seriously. "What's on your mind, Tom?"

"Nothing. Nothing that I know of." But the boy's hand shook so much that he spilled his coffee.

"And you really do say such nonsense," Sid said. "Last night you kept saying, 'It's blood, it's blood, that's what it is!' You repeated that over and over. And you said, 'Don't torture me like this—I'll tell!' Tell what? What exactly will you tell?"

Everything was spinning around Tom. There's no way to know what might have happened next, but fortunately the worry disappeared from Aunt Polly's face and she unknowingly came to Tom's rescue. She said:

"Wow! It's that terrible murder. I dream about it almost every night myself. Sometimes I dream that I'm the one who did it."

Mary said she had been affected in much the same way. Sid seemed satisfied with this response. Tom left as quickly as he reasonably could, and for the next week he complained about having a toothache, wrapping up his jaw every night before bed. He had no idea that Sid stayed awake each night watching him, often carefully removing the bandage and then propping himself up on his elbow to listen for long periods at a time, before quietly putting the bandage back in place. Tom's mental distress gradually faded away and the fake toothache became annoying, so he stopped pretending. If Sid actually managed to understand anything from Tom's fragmented mumbling during sleep, he kept whatever he learned to himself.

It felt to Tom like his classmates would never stop conducting investigations into dead cats, constantly reminding him of his troubles. Sid observed that Tom never served as the leader during these examinations, even though he usually took charge of any new activities. Sid also noticed that Tom never participated as a witness, which seemed odd. Additionally, Sid didn't miss the fact that Tom clearly disliked these investigations and avoided them whenever possible. Sid found this puzzling but kept his thoughts to himself. Eventually, however, these investigations fell out of fashion and stopped tormenting Tom's guilty conscience.

Every day or two during this sorrowful period, Tom looked for his chance and made his way to the small barred jail window, sneaking whatever little comforts he could find through to the "murderer." The jail was a small, insignificant brick structure that sat in a swamp at the village's edge, with no guards assigned to watch it; in fact, it was rarely used. These gestures of kindness did much to relieve Tom's guilty conscience.

The villagers desperately wanted to tar and feather Injun Joe and run him out of town on a rail for stealing corpses, but his reputation was so intimidating that no one was brave enough to step forward and lead the charge, so they abandoned the idea. He had been smart enough to start both of his testimony statements with the fight, without admitting to the grave robbing that happened before it; as a result, it was considered best not to take the case to court right now.

Chapter XII

One of the reasons Tom's mind had wandered away from his secret troubles was that it had discovered a new and serious matter to occupy itself with. Becky Thatcher had stopped attending school. Tom had wrestled with his pride for several days and attempted to "whistle her down the wind," but he failed. He started finding himself loitering around her father's house at night, feeling extremely miserable. She was sick. What if she died! The thought was deeply disturbing. He no longer showed interest in war or even piracy. Life's appeal had vanished; nothing remained but gloom. He stored away his hoop and his bat; they brought him no happiness anymore. His aunt grew worried. She started testing all sorts of treatments on him. She belonged to that group of people who are obsessed with patent medicines and all newfangled approaches to creating health or restoring it. She was a persistent experimenter with these remedies. Whenever something new in this field appeared, she immediately became eager to test it; not on herself, since she was never sick, but on anyone else who happened to be available. She subscribed to all the "Health" magazines and phrenological scams; and the serious ignorance they promoted was like fresh air to her. All the nonsense they published about ventilation, how to sleep, how to wake up, what to eat, what to drink, how much exercise to get, what mental state to maintain, and what kind of clothes to wear was absolute truth to her, and she never noticed that her health magazines each month typically contradicted everything they had suggested the previous month. She was as innocent and sincere as could be, which made her an easy target. She collected her fraudulent magazines and her fraudulent medicines, and armed with death in this way, she went around on her pale horse, figuratively speaking, with "hell following after." However, she never realized that she wasn't an angel of healing and the balm of Gilead in disguise to her suffering neighbors.

The water treatment was a new approach, and Tom's poor health was exactly what she needed to try it out. Every morning at dawn, she would drag him out to the woodshed and completely soak him with a flood of ice-cold water. After that, she would scrub him down with a towel that felt like sandpaper, which would wake him up completely. Then she would wrap him tightly in a wet sheet and tuck him under heavy blankets until he sweated so much that his soul felt purified and "the yellow stains of it came through his pores"—at least that's how Tom described it.

Despite all these efforts, the boy became increasingly sad, pale, and downcast. She introduced hot baths, sitz baths, shower baths, and cold plunges. The boy stayed as gloomy as a funeral procession. She started supplementing the water treatments with a meager oatmeal diet and medicinal plasters that raised blisters. She measured his capacity like she would a pitcher's, and stuffed him full every day with questionable remedies.

By this point, Tom had grown completely indifferent to any form of punishment. This attitude deeply troubled the elderly woman and filled her with worry. She knew this indifference had to be eliminated no matter what it took. It was then that she first learned about Pain-killer. She immediately ordered a large supply. After tasting it herself, she felt overwhelmed with thankfulness. The medicine was essentially liquid fire. She abandoned the water treatment and all other remedies, placing her complete trust in Pain-killer instead. She gave Tom a teaspoonful and watched anxiously for his reaction. Her worries disappeared immediately, and her mind was at ease once more, because his "indifference" had been completely shattered. The boy couldn't have displayed more intense, enthusiastic interest even if she had literally set a fire beneath him.

Tom realized it was time to snap out of it; this kind of life might seem romantic enough given his miserable state, but it was starting to lack emotion and have too much confusing chaos. So he considered different plans to get out of this situation, and eventually came up with the idea of pretending to like Pain-killer. He requested it so frequently that he became annoying, and his aunt finally told him to take it himself and stop pestering her. If it had been Sid, she wouldn't have had any doubts to dampen her happiness; but because it was Tom, she secretly kept an eye on the bottle. She discovered that the medicine was actually decreasing, but it never crossed her mind that the boy was using it to fix a crack in the sitting-room floor.

One day Tom was in the middle of taking his medicine when his aunt's yellow cat wandered over, purring and staring greedily at the teaspoon, begging for a taste. Tom said:

"Don't ask for it unless you want it, Peter."

But Peter indicated that he did want it.

"You better make sure."

Peter was certain.

"Now you've asked for it, and I'll give it to you, because there's nothing mean about me; but if you find you don't like it, you can't blame anybody but yourself."

Peter was willing. So Tom forced his mouth open and poured the medicine down his throat. Peter shot a couple of yards into the air, then let out a wild cry and began racing around and around the room, crashing into furniture, knocking over flower pots, and creating complete chaos. Then he stood up on his back legs and danced around in wild delight, his head thrown back over his shoulder while his voice announced his overwhelming joy. After that he went tearing through the house again, leaving destruction and mayhem in his wake. Aunt Polly came in just in time to watch him perform a few somersaults, give one last tremendous shout, and leap through the open window, taking the remaining flower pots with him. The old woman stood frozen in amazement, looking over her spectacles; Tom lay on the floor dying with laughter.

"Tom, what in the world is wrong with that cat?"

"I don't know, aunt," the boy gasped.

"Why, I've never seen anything like it. What made him act that way?"

"I really don't know, Aunt Polly; cats always act like that when they're having a good time."

"They do, do they?" There was something in his tone that made Tom uneasy.

"Yes, ma'am. That is, I believe they do."

"You do?"

"Yes'm."

The elderly woman was leaning over, with Tom observing her, his curiosity mixed with growing worry. He realized her intention too late. The handle of the revealing teaspoon could be seen beneath the bed skirt. Aunt Polly picked it up and held it in the air. Tom flinched and looked away. Aunt Polly grabbed him by her usual method—his ear—and gave his head a solid knock with her thimble.

"Now, sir, why did you want to treat that poor helpless animal like that?"

"I did it out of pity for him—because he didn't have any aunt."

"Didn't have any aunt!—you idiot. What does that have to do with anything?"

"Absolutely. Because if he'd had one, she would have burned him out herself! She would have roasted his insides without any more feeling than if he was human!"

Aunt Polly suddenly felt a sharp stab of guilt. This put things in a completely different perspective; what would be cruel to a cat could also be cruel to a boy. She started to relent; she felt regret. Her eyes began to well up with tears, and she gently placed her hand on Tom's head and said softly:

"I was trying to do what was best for you, Tom. And, Tom, it really did help you."

Tom glanced up at her face with just a barely noticeable sparkle showing through his serious expression.

"I know you meant well, aunt, and I did too with Peter. It did him some good as well. I haven't seen him move around so much since—"

"Oh, go away, Tom, before you make me angry again. And try to see if you can be a good boy for once, and you won't need to take any more medicine."

Tom arrived at school early. People had noticed that this unusual behavior had been happening every day recently. And now, as had become his habit lately, he lingered around the schoolyard gate instead of playing with his friends. He claimed he was sick, and he certainly appeared to be. He pretended to look everywhere except where he was actually looking—down the road. Soon Jeff Thatcher came into view, and Tom's face brightened; he stared for a moment, then turned away sadly. When Jeff arrived, Tom approached him and carefully steered the conversation toward opportunities to mention Becky, but the carefree boy never took the hint. Tom kept watching and waiting, his hopes rising whenever he spotted a girl's dress approaching, then immediately disliking whoever it was once he realized she wasn't the right person. Finally, no more girls appeared, and he sank hopelessly into despair; he entered the empty schoolhouse and sat down to wallow in his misery. Then another dress appeared at the gate, and Tom's heart leaped. The next moment he was outside, acting wild like a Native American warrior; shouting, laughing, chasing boys, jumping over the fence dangerously, doing cartwheels, standing on his head—performing every impressive feat he could think of, while secretly watching to see if Becky Thatcher was paying attention. But she seemed completely unaware of his performance;

she never even glanced his way. Was it possible that she didn't realize he was there? He moved his stunts closer to where she stood; came whooping around like a warrior, grabbed a boy's hat, threw it onto the schoolhouse roof, charged through a group of boys, knocking them down in all directions, and fell flat on his face right in front of Becky, nearly knocking her over—and she turned away with her nose in the air, and he heard her say: "Hmph! Some people think they're so clever—always showing off!"

Tom's face flushed with embarrassment. He pulled himself together and slipped away, feeling defeated and humiliated.

Chapter XIII

Tom had made his decision. He felt miserable and hopeless. He was an abandoned boy with no friends, he told himself; no one cared about him; when people discovered what they had pushed him toward, maybe they would feel regret; he had attempted to behave properly and fit in, but they wouldn't allow him to; since they wanted nothing more than to get rid of him, so be it; and they could hold him responsible for what happened next—why shouldn't they? What right did someone without friends have to object? Yes, they had finally forced his hand: he would live as a criminal. He had no other option.

By this time he was far down Meadow Lane, and the school bell signaling time to "take up" rang faintly in his ears. He sobbed now, thinking he would never, ever hear that old familiar sound again—it was incredibly difficult, but he had no choice; since he was being forced out into the harsh world, he had to accept it—but he forgave them. Then the sobs came in rapid succession.

Just then he encountered his closest friend, Joe Harper—with a stern expression and clearly carrying some heavy, gloomy intention in his heart. Obviously here were two people thinking exactly the same thing. Tom, wiping his eyes with his sleeve, started to sob out something about his decision to escape from harsh treatment and lack of understanding at home by wandering off into the wide world never to come back; and finished by hoping that Joe wouldn't forget him.

But it turned out that this was exactly what Joe had been planning to ask Tom, and he had come looking for him for that very reason. His mother had beaten him for drinking some cream that he had never even tasted and knew nothing about; it was obvious that she was fed up with him and wanted him to leave; if that's how she felt, he had no choice but to give in; he hoped she would be happy and never feel sorry for forcing her poor boy out into the cold, harsh world to suffer and die.

As the two boys walked sadly together, they made a fresh agreement to support each other and remain brothers, never parting until death freed them from their troubles. Then they started making their plans. Joe wanted to become a hermit, surviving on bread crusts in a distant cave, and eventually dying from cold, hunger, and sorrow; but after hearing Tom's arguments, he admitted that a criminal life had some obvious benefits, so he agreed to become a pirate instead.

Three miles downstream from St. Petersburg, where the Mississippi River stretched just over a mile wide, there stood a long, narrow, tree-covered island with a shallow sandbar at its tip, making it an ideal meeting place. No one lived there, and it sat far toward the opposite shore, next to a thick forest that was almost completely uninhabited. This is why they selected Jackson's Island. The question of who would become the targets of their pirate raids never crossed their minds. Next, they tracked down Huckleberry Finn, who eagerly agreed to join them right away, since any adventure appealed to him equally—he didn't care what they did. Soon after, they split up, planning to meet at an isolated spot along the riverbank two miles upstream from the village at their preferred time—midnight. A small log raft waited there, which they intended to steal. Each boy would bring fishing hooks and line, along with whatever food he could sneak away in the most secretive and mysterious manner possible—just as real outlaws would do. Before the afternoon ended, they had all savored the delicious thrill of hinting around town that people would soon "hear something big." Everyone who received this mysterious clue was warned to "keep quiet and wait."

Around midnight, Tom showed up carrying a boiled ham and some small items, then took cover in thick brush on a little hill that looked down over the meeting spot. The stars were out, and everything was completely quiet. The huge river stretched out like a calm ocean. Tom paused to listen for a moment, but nothing broke the silence. Then he let out a soft, clear whistle. Someone answered from below the hill. Tom whistled two more times, and these signals got the same response. Then a careful voice spoke:

"Who goes there?"

"Tom Sawyer, the Black Avenger of the Spanish Main. Tell me your names."

"Huck Finn the Red-Handed, and Joe Harper the Terror of the Seas." Tom had come up with these titles from his favorite books.

"'Tis well. Give the countersign."

Two raspy whispers spoke the same terrible word at exactly the same moment into the dark, contemplative night:

"Blood!"

Then Tom threw his ham over the cliff and climbed down after it, scraping his skin and tearing his clothes somewhat in the process. There was a simple, easy path along the shore below the cliff, but it didn't offer the challenges and risks that a pirate treasured so much.

The Terror of the Seas had brought a side of bacon and had nearly exhausted himself getting it to their destination. Finn the Red-Handed had stolen a frying pan and a good amount of partially cured tobacco leaves, and had also brought several corn cobs to fashion into pipes. However, none of the pirates smoked or chewed tobacco except for him. The Black Avenger of the Spanish Main declared that they absolutely couldn't begin without fire. This was smart thinking, since matches were virtually unknown in those times. They spotted a fire burning on a large raft about a hundred yards upstream, so they crept over quietly and took a burning piece for themselves. They turned it into a dramatic adventure, whispering "Hist!" from time to time and suddenly stopping with fingers pressed to their lips, moving with hands resting on imaginary sword handles, and giving commands in hushed, ominous whispers that if "the enemy" made any movement, they should "run him through completely," since "dead men tell no tales." They were perfectly aware that all the raft workers had gone down to the village to buy supplies or enjoy themselves, but that still didn't justify handling this operation in anything less than a proper pirate manner.

They pushed off from shore, with Tom taking charge, Huck handling the rear oar and Joe working the front one. Tom positioned himself in the middle of the boat, his brow furrowed with a dark expression, arms crossed, issuing his commands in a quiet, serious whisper:

"Turn into the wind and bring her around!"

"Yes, sir!"

"Steady, steady-y-y-y!"

"It's steady, sir!"

"Let her sail off course a bit!"

"That's exactly the point, sir!"

As the boys steadily and monotonously steered the raft toward the middle of the stream, it was clearly understood that these commands were given only for show and weren't meant to have any real meaning.

"What sails is she carrying?"

"Courses, topsails, and flying jib, sir."

"Send the royal sails up! Climb aloft there, half a dozen of you—fore topgallant studding sail! Move quickly, now!"

"Yes, sir!"

"Shake out that main topgallant sail! Sheets and braces! Now my hearties!"

"Yes, sir!"

"Hellum-a-lee—hard a port! Stand by to meet her when she comes! Port, port! Now, men! With a will! Stead-y-y-y!"

"It's steady, sir!"

The raft moved past the middle of the river; the boys pointed it in the right direction, and then rested on their oars. The river wasn't running high, so there was only a two or three mile current. Barely a word was spoken during the next forty-five minutes. Now the raft was floating past the distant town. Two or three flickering lights showed where it rested, sleeping peacefully, beyond the dim vast expanse of star-studded water, unaware of the tremendous event that was taking place. The Black Avenger stood motionless with his arms crossed, "taking his final look" at the scene of his former happiness and his recent troubles, and wishing "she" could see him now, out on the wild sea, facing danger and death with a fearless heart, going to his fate with a grim smile on his face. It took only a small stretch of his imagination to picture Jackson's Island as being beyond sight of the village, and so he "took his final look" with a broken yet satisfied heart. The other pirates were taking their final looks, too; and they all stared so long that they nearly let the current carry them out of range of the island. But they noticed the danger in time, and managed to prevent it.

Around two o'clock in the morning the raft ran aground on the sandbar two hundred yards above the tip of the island, and they waded back and forth until they had unloaded their cargo. Part of the small raft's supplies included an old sail, and this they stretched over a hollow in the bushes to make a tent for sheltering their food; but they themselves would sleep under the open sky in fair weather, as proper outlaws should.

They built a fire next to a large fallen log about twenty or thirty steps deep into the dark forest, then cooked some bacon in their frying pan for dinner and ate half of the cornbread they had packed. It felt like an amazing adventure to be eating this way in the wild, completely free in the untouched forest of an unexplored and empty island, far away from other people, and they declared they would never go back to civilization. The dancing flames illuminated their faces and cast a warm red glow on the tall tree trunks of their natural cathedral, and on the glossy leaves and hanging vines all around them.

When the final crispy piece of bacon had been eaten and the last portion of cornbread consumed, the boys lay down on the grass, completely satisfied. They could have located a cooler spot, but they refused to give up such a romantic element as the blazing campfire.

"Isn't it wonderful?" said Joe.

"This is crazy!" Tom said. "What would the guys say if they could see us?"

"Say? Well, they'd just die to be here—hey, Hucky!"

"I think so," said Huckleberry; "anyway, I'm satisfied. I don't want anything better than this. I don't ever get enough to eat, usually—and here they can't come and bother a person and hassle him like that."

"It's exactly the life I want," Tom said. "You don't need to wake up early in the morning, and you don't need to attend school, or wash up, or deal with all that ridiculous nonsense. You see, when a pirate comes ashore, Joe, he doesn't have to do anything at all, but a hermit has to spend a lot of time praying, and besides, he doesn't get to have any fun since he's all alone like that."

"Oh yes, that's true," said Joe, "but I hadn't really thought much about it, you know. I'd much rather be a pirate, now that I've tried it."

"You see," said Tom, "people don't really care about hermits these days like they did back in the old times, but a pirate is always respected. And a hermit has to sleep on the hardest surface he can find, and put rough cloth and ashes on his head, and stand out in the rain, and—"

"Why does he put sackcloth and ashes on his head?" asked Huck.

"I don't know. But they have to do it. Hermits always do. You'd have to do that if you were a hermit."

"I sure wouldn't," said Huck.

"Well, what would you do?"

"I don't know. But I wouldn't do that."

"Why, Huck, you'd have to. How would you get around it?"

"Why, I just wouldn't stand it. I'd run away."

"Run away! Well, you would be a pathetic excuse for a hermit. You'd be a complete disgrace."

The Red-Handed didn't respond, being busy with more important matters. He had finished hollowing out a corncob, and now he attached a weed stem to it, filled it with tobacco, and was holding a glowing coal to the mixture while puffing out a cloud of sweet-smelling smoke—he was experiencing complete and luxurious satisfaction. The other pirates were jealous of his impressive habit, and quietly decided they would learn to do it soon. After a moment Huck said:

"What do pirates have to do?"

Tom said:

"Oh, they have an amazing time—they capture ships and burn them, and take the money and bury it in terrible places on their island where there are ghosts and other things to guard it, and they kill everyone on the ships—they make them walk the plank."

"And they take the women to the island," said Joe; "they don't kill the women."

"No," Tom agreed, "they don't kill the women—they're too noble. And the women are always beautiful, too."

"And don't they wear the most amazing clothes! Oh no! All gold and silver and diamonds," said Joe, with enthusiasm.

"Who?" said Huck.

"Why, the pirates."

Huck looked down at his own clothes with a feeling of hopelessness.

"I suppose I'm not dressed properly for a pirate," he said, with regretful sadness in his voice; "but these are all the clothes I have."

The other boys assured him that fine clothes would come quickly once they started their adventures. They explained that his worn-out clothes would be sufficient to begin with, even though wealthy pirates typically started out with a proper wardrobe.

Gradually their conversation faded away and sleepiness began to creep over the eyelids of the little outcasts. The pipe slipped from the Red-Handed's fingers, and he fell into the deep sleep of those who are both exhausted and free from guilt. The Terror of the Seas and the Black Avenger of the Spanish Main found it harder to fall asleep. They whispered their prayers silently to themselves, then lay down, since no one was there with the authority to make them kneel and pray out loud; honestly, they were tempted not to say their prayers at all, but they were too scared to go that far, worried they might bring down a sudden bolt of lightning from heaven as punishment. Then they quickly reached the edge of sleep and hovered there—but an unwelcome visitor arrived that wouldn't go away. It was their conscience. They started to feel a nagging worry that they had done something wrong by running away; then they remembered the stolen meat, and that's when the real agony began. They tried to reason away their guilt by reminding their conscience that they had stolen candy and apples countless times before; but their conscience wouldn't be satisfied with such weak excuses; it seemed to them, in the end, that there was no way around the undeniable truth that taking candy was just "swiping," while taking bacon and ham and other valuable items was plain and simple theft—and the Bible had a commandment against that. So they silently decided that as long as they stayed in this line of work, their pirate activities would never again be tainted with the sin of stealing. Then their conscience called a temporary ceasefire, and these strangely contradictory pirates drifted peacefully off to sleep.

Chapter XIV

When Tom woke up in the morning, he wondered where he was. He sat up and rubbed his eyes and looked around. Then he understood. It was the cool gray dawn, and there was a wonderful feeling of rest and peace in the deep, all-encompassing calm and silence of the woods. Not a single leaf moved; not a sound interrupted nature's quiet meditation. Tiny dewdrops sparkled on the leaves and grass. A white layer of ashes covered the fire, and a thin blue wisp of smoke rose straight up into the air. Joe and Huck were still sleeping.

Now, far away in the woods a bird called out; another bird answered back; soon the hammering of a woodpecker could be heard. Slowly the cool, dim gray of the morning grew brighter, and gradually sounds increased and life began to show itself. The wonder of Nature waking up from sleep and starting its daily work revealed itself to the thoughtful boy. A small green worm came crawling across a dew-covered leaf, raising two-thirds of its body into the air from time to time and "sniffing around," then moving forward again—because it was measuring, Tom explained; and when the worm approached him on its own, he sat as motionless as a stone, with his hopes rising and falling in turns, as the creature continued coming toward him or seemed ready to go somewhere else; and when finally it paused for a difficult moment with its curved body in the air and then came decisively down onto Tom's leg and began a journey across him, his whole heart filled with joy—because that meant he was going to get a new suit of clothes—without any doubt a flashy pirate outfit. Then a line of ants appeared from nowhere in particular and went about their work; one struggled bravely along with a dead spider five times larger than itself in its grip, and dragged it straight up a tree trunk. A brown spotted ladybug climbed the dizzying height of a grass blade, and Tom leaned down close to it and said, "Ladybug, ladybug, fly away home, your house is on fire, your children are alone," and she spread her wings and flew off to check on it—which didn't surprise the boy, because he knew from experience that this insect was easily fooled about fires, and he had taken advantage of its gullibility more than once. A dung beetle came next, pushing steadily at its ball, and Tom touched the creature to watch it pull its legs against its body and pretend to be dead. The birds were making quite a commotion by this time. A catbird, the Northern mockingbird, landed in a tree above Tom's head and sang out her imitations of her neighbors in a burst of delight; then a loud jay swooped down like a flash of blue flame and perched on a branch almost within the boy's reach, tilted his head to one side and studied the strangers with intense curiosity; a gray squirrel and a large "fox" squirrel came scampering along, sitting up at intervals to examine and chatter at the boys, because the wild animals had probably never seen a human being before and hardly knew whether to be frightened or not. All of Nature was fully awake and active now; long beams of sunlight broke through the thick leaves far and near, and a few butterflies came dancing onto the scene.

Tom roused the other pirates and they all rushed off with a yell, and within a minute or two had stripped off their clothes and were chasing each other and tumbling around in the clear, shallow water of the white sandbar. They felt no yearning for the small village that lay sleeping in the distance beyond the vast expanse of water. A wandering current or a small rise in the river had swept away their raft, but this only pleased them, since losing it was like burning the bridge that connected them to civilization.

They returned to camp feeling wonderfully refreshed, happy, and extremely hungry, and they quickly got the campfire burning brightly again. Huck discovered a spring of clear, cold water nearby, and the boys fashioned cups from wide oak or hickory leaves, feeling that water enhanced with such natural wilderness magic would serve as an excellent replacement for coffee. While Joe was cutting bacon for breakfast, Tom and Huck told him to wait a moment; they walked to a promising spot along the riverbank and cast their fishing lines; almost instantly they were rewarded with catches. Joe hadn't had time to grow impatient before they returned with some beautiful bass, a couple of sunfish, and a small catfish—enough food for quite a large group. They cooked the fish alongside the bacon and were amazed; no fish had ever tasted so wonderful before. They didn't realize that the sooner a freshwater fish gets cooked after being caught, the better it tastes; and they gave little thought to what an amazing seasoning outdoor sleeping, outdoor activity, swimming, and a hefty dose of hunger provide as well.

They lounged in the shade after breakfast while Huck smoked, then headed into the woods to explore. They walked cheerfully along, stepping over rotting logs, pushing through thick undergrowth, and moving among the majestic old trees that were draped from their tops to the forest floor with cascading grape vines. Occasionally they discovered cozy spots covered with soft grass and dotted with colorful flowers.

They found plenty of things to enjoy, but nothing that truly amazed them. They discovered the island stretched about three miles long and a quarter of a mile wide, with the nearest shore separated by only a narrow channel barely two hundred yards across. They went swimming about every hour, so it was nearly mid-afternoon when they returned to camp. They were too hungry to bother fishing, but they feasted on cold ham before collapsing in the shade to chat. However, the conversation soon started to slow down and eventually stopped altogether. The quiet, the serious atmosphere that hung over the woods, and the feeling of being alone began to affect the boys' moods. They started thinking deeply. A kind of vague yearning came over them. This feeling gradually took shape—it was the beginning of homesickness. Even Finn the Red-Handed found himself thinking about his doorsteps and empty barrels. But they were all embarrassed by their weakness, and none had the courage to voice what he was thinking.

For quite a while now, the boys had been dimly aware of an unusual sound coming from far away, much like how someone might notice a clock ticking without really paying attention to it. But now this strange sound grew louder and demanded their attention. The boys jumped, looked at one another, and then each took on a listening posture. A long silence followed, deep and complete; then a low, ominous rumble drifted toward them from the distance.

"What is it!" Joe whispered urgently.

"I wonder," Tom whispered.

""It's not thunder," said Huckleberry, in an awed tone, "because thunder—"

"Listen!" said Tom. "Pay attention—don't talk."

They waited for what felt like an eternity, and then the same muted explosion disturbed the profound silence.

"Let's go and see."

They jumped up and rushed toward the shore in the direction of the town. They pushed through the bushes along the bank and looked out across the water. The small steam ferry was about a mile downstream from the village, floating along with the current. Its wide deck appeared packed with people. Many small boats were rowing around or drifting with the flow near the ferry, but the boys couldn't figure out what the men in those boats were doing. Suddenly, a large burst of white smoke shot out from the ferry's side, and as it spread and drifted upward in a slow-moving cloud, that same muffled booming sound reached the listeners once more.

"I know now!" Tom shouted; "someone has drowned!"

"That's it!" said Huck. "They did that last summer when Bill Turner drowned. They fire a cannon over the water, and that makes the body come up to the surface. Yes, and they take loaves of bread and put mercury in them and set them floating, and wherever there's anybody who's drowned, the bread will float right there and stop."

"Yes, I've heard about that," Joe said. "I wonder what causes the bread to do that."

"Oh, it's not really about the bread," said Tom; "I think it's mostly about what they say over it before they send it out."

"But they don't say anything over it," said Huck. "I've seen them and they don't."

"Well, that's funny," Tom said. "But maybe they say it to themselves. Of course they do. Anyone could figure that out."

The other boys agreed that Tom's reasoning made sense, because a simple piece of bread, without the guidance of a magical spell, couldn't be expected to perform very smartly when given such an important task.

"Wow, I really wish I was over there right now," said Joe.

"I do too," said Huck. "I'd give anything to know who it is."

The boys continued to listen and watch. Suddenly, an enlightening thought struck Tom, and he called out:

"Boys, I know who's drowned—it's us!"

They felt like heroes right away. This was an amazing victory; people were missing them; they were being mourned; hearts were breaking because of them; tears were flowing; guilty memories of being mean to these poor lost boys were coming back, and people were feeling useless regret and remorse; and most importantly, the departed were what everyone in town was talking about, and all the other boys were jealous of this incredible fame. This was wonderful. Being a pirate was definitely worth it, after all.

As evening approached, the ferryboat returned to its regular duties and the small boats vanished. The pirates went back to their camp. They were filled with pride over their newfound importance and the remarkable commotion they were causing. They caught fish, prepared dinner and ate it, and then began speculating about what the village was thinking and saying about them; the images they conjured of the public distress caused by their disappearance were satisfying to contemplate—from their perspective. But when the darkness of night surrounded them, they slowly stopped talking and sat staring into the fire, their thoughts clearly drifting somewhere else. The thrill had faded now, and Tom and Joe couldn't push away thoughts of certain people back home who weren't enjoying this exciting adventure as much as they were. Doubts crept in; they became worried and miserable; a sigh or two slipped out without them realizing it. Eventually Joe cautiously attempted an indirect suggestion about how the others might feel regarding a return to civilization—not immediately, but—

Tom crushed him with scorn! Huck, who hadn't taken sides yet, joined forces with Tom, and the hesitant boy quickly offered his "explanation," relieved to escape the situation with as little evidence of cowardly homesickness attached to his reputation as possible. The rebellion was effectively put down for the time being.

As the night grew darker, Huck started to doze off and soon began snoring. Joe was the next to fall asleep. Tom remained lying on his elbow without moving for quite some time, watching both of them carefully. Finally, he slowly and quietly got up on his knees and began searching through the grass and the dancing shadows cast by the campfire. He picked up and examined several large curved pieces of thin white bark from a sycamore tree, eventually selecting two that seemed right for his purpose. Then he knelt beside the fire and carefully wrote something on each piece of bark with his "red keel"; he rolled one up and placed it in his jacket pocket, while putting the other in Joe's hat and moving it some distance away from its sleeping owner. He also placed in the hat certain schoolboy treasures of nearly priceless value—including a piece of chalk, a rubber ball, three fishhooks, and one of those special marbles called a "sure 'nough crystal." Then he carefully tiptoed through the trees until he was confident he was beyond hearing range, and immediately began running swiftly toward the sandbar.

Chapter XV

A few minutes later, Tom found himself in the shallow water near the sandbar, making his way toward the Illinois shore. By the time the water reached his waist, he was already halfway across; the current was too strong for any more wading, so he confidently began swimming the remaining hundred yards. He swam at an angle upstream, but the current still carried him downstream faster than he had anticipated. Nevertheless, he eventually reached the shore and drifted along until he discovered a low spot where he could pull himself out. He checked his jacket pocket with his hand, confirmed his piece of bark was still safe, and then made his way through the woods, following the shoreline with his clothes dripping wet. Just before ten o'clock, he emerged into a clearing across from the village and spotted the ferryboat resting in the shadow of the trees and the steep riverbank. Everything lay silent beneath the twinkling stars. He carefully crept down the bank, keeping his eyes alert for any movement, slipped quietly into the water, took three or four strokes, and climbed into the small boat that served as the ferryboat's tender at the stern. He lay down beneath the rowing seats and waited, breathing heavily.

Soon the damaged bell rang and a voice called out the command to "cast off." A minute or two afterward, the small boat's front end was positioned high against the steamboat's wake, and the journey had started. Tom was pleased with his accomplishment, since he understood this would be the vessel's final voyage of the evening. After a lengthy twelve to fifteen minutes, the paddle wheels came to a halt, and Tom quietly slipped into the water and swam to shore in the twilight, coming ashore fifty yards downriver, safely away from any potential lingering passengers.

He raced through empty side streets and soon reached his aunt's backyard fence. He climbed over it, walked up to the house extension, and peered through the sitting-room window where a lamp was glowing. Inside sat Aunt Polly, Sid, Mary, and Joe Harper's mother, sitting close together in conversation. They had gathered near the bed, which stood between them and the door. Tom approached the door and carefully began lifting the latch; then he pushed gently until the door opened just a crack; he kept pushing slowly and cautiously, trembling each time it squeaked, until he figured he could crawl through on his knees; so he stuck his head through the opening and began moving forward carefully.

"What's making the candle flicker like that?" asked Aunt Polly. Tom quickly moved closer. "Oh, that door is open, I think. Yes, of course it is. So many odd things happening lately. Go ahead and close it, Sid."

Tom slipped under the bed just in time. He lay there catching his breath for a while, then crawled to a spot where he could nearly reach his aunt's foot.

"But as I was saying," said Aunt Polly, "he wasn't bad, really—just mischievous. Only playful and reckless, you know. He wasn't any more responsible than a young horse. He never meant any harm, and he was the most kind-hearted boy that ever lived"—and she began to cry.

"That's exactly how my Joe was—always full of mischief and getting into every kind of trouble, but he was as unselfish and kind as anyone could be—and goodness gracious, to think I went and spanked him for taking that cream, never once remembering that I had thrown it out myself because it had gone sour, and now I'll never see him again in this world, never, never, never, my poor mistreated boy!" And Mrs. Harper cried as if her heart would shatter.

"I hope Tom's in a better place now," said Sid, "but if he had been better in some ways—"

"Sid!" Tom could feel the old woman's fierce stare, even though he couldn't see it. "Don't say a word against my Tom, now that he's gone! God will take care of him—don't you worry about that, sir! Oh, Mrs. Harper, I don't know how to let him go! I don't know how to let him go! He brought me such comfort, even though he nearly worried my old heart to death."

"The Lord gives and the Lord has taken away—Blessed be the name of the Lord! But it's so difficult—Oh, it's so difficult! Just last Saturday my Joe set off a firecracker right under my nose and I knocked him down. I had no idea then how soon—Oh, if I could do it over again I'd hug him and bless him for it."

"Yes, yes, yes, I know exactly how you feel, Mrs. Harper, I know precisely how you feel. Just yesterday at noon, my Tom went and filled the cat with Pain-killer, and I thought that creature was going to tear the whole house apart. And may God forgive me, I hit Tom on the head with my thimble, poor boy, my poor dead boy. But he's free from all his troubles now. And the last words I ever heard him speak were meant to scold—"

But this memory overwhelmed the elderly woman completely, and she broke down entirely. Tom was now sniffling as well—though more out of self-pity than sympathy for anyone else. He could hear Mary weeping and occasionally speaking kindly on his behalf. He started to think more highly of himself than he ever had before. Even so, his aunt's sorrow moved him enough that he wanted to burst out from beneath the bed and fill her with happiness—the dramatic spectacle of such a scene also strongly attracted his theatrical nature, but he held back and remained motionless.

He continued listening and pieced together from various fragments that people initially thought the boys had drowned while swimming; then someone noticed the small raft was missing; after that, certain boys mentioned that the missing kids had promised the village would "hear something" soon; the local experts had "connected the dots" and concluded that the boys had taken off on that raft and would show up in the next town downstream shortly; but around midday the raft was discovered, stuck against the Missouri riverbank about five or six miles below the village—and at that point hope died; they had to be drowned, otherwise hunger would have forced them to return home by evening if not earlier. People believed that searching for the bodies had been pointless simply because the drowning must have happened in the middle of the river, since the boys, being strong swimmers, would have made it to shore otherwise. This was Wednesday night. If the bodies remained missing until Sunday, all hope would be abandoned, and the funeral services would be held that morning. Tom trembled.

Mrs. Harper said a tearful goodnight and started to leave. Then, moved by the same instinct, both grieving women threw themselves into each other's arms and shared a good, comforting cry before saying goodbye. Aunt Polly was much more gentle than usual when she said goodnight to Sid and Mary. Sid sniffled quietly while Mary walked away sobbing her heart out.

Aunt Polly knelt down and prayed for Tom with such deep emotion and heartfelt appeal, her words filled with boundless love and her elderly voice trembling, that he was drowning in tears again long before she finished.

He had to remain motionless long after she went to bed, because she kept making heartbroken cries from time to time, tossing restlessly, and turning over. But finally she was quiet, only whimpering a little in her sleep. Now the boy crept out, slowly rose by the bedside, blocked the candlelight with his hand, and stood looking at her. His heart was filled with compassion for her. He pulled out his sycamore scroll and set it by the candle. But something came to him, and he hesitated thinking. His face brightened with a joyful answer to his thoughts; he quickly put the bark in his pocket. Then he leaned over and kissed the worn lips, and immediately made his quiet escape, fastening the door behind him.

He made his way back to the ferry dock, found no one around, and boldly walked onto the boat, knowing it was empty except for a watchman who always went to bed and slept like a stone statue. He untied the small boat at the back, climbed into it, and soon began rowing carefully upstream. After he had rowed about a mile past the village, he started crossing diagonally and put all his strength into the work. He reached the landing on the opposite side perfectly, since this was something he had done many times before. He considered taking the small boat with him, thinking it could be seen as a ship and therefore fair game for a pirate, but he realized they would search thoroughly for it and that could lead to discoveries. So he stepped onto shore and went into the woods.

He sat down and took a long rest, struggling to stay awake the entire time, then cautiously began the final leg of his journey home. The night was nearly over. Dawn had fully broken by the time he reached the sandbar alongside the island. He rested once more until the sun climbed high and bathed the mighty river in golden light, then he dove into the water. Shortly afterward, he stood dripping on the edge of the campsite and heard Joe speaking:

"No, Tom is completely loyal, Huck, and he'll return. He won't abandon us. He understands that would bring shame to a pirate, and Tom has too much pride for that kind of behavior. He's planning something or another. Now I'm curious what it could be?"

"Well, the things are ours anyway, aren't they?"

"Pretty close, but not quite yet, Huck. The note says they will if he doesn't come back here for breakfast."

"And that's exactly what he is!" Tom declared with impressive theatrical flair, striding magnificently into the camp.

A lavish breakfast of bacon and fish was soon prepared, and while the boys dug into their meal, Tom told his story, adding extra details to make it sound even better. By the time he finished his tale, they all felt like proud and boastful heroes. Afterward, Tom found a cool, shaded spot to nap until noon, while the other pirates prepared to go fishing and exploring.

Chapter XVI

After dinner, the entire group went out to search for turtle eggs on the sandbar. They walked around jabbing sticks into the sand, and whenever they discovered a soft spot, they dropped to their knees and dug with their hands. Occasionally they would pull fifty or sixty eggs from a single hole. The eggs were perfectly round, white objects slightly smaller than an English walnut. They enjoyed a wonderful fried-egg feast that evening, and had another one on Friday morning.

After breakfast they went whooping and dancing out onto the sandbar, chasing each other in circles while stripping off their clothes as they ran, until they were completely naked, then continued their playful antics far up into the shallow water of the sandbar, fighting against the strong current that occasionally swept their feet out from under them and made the game even more entertaining. Every so often they would gather in a cluster and splash water at each other's faces with their hands, slowly moving closer together while turning their heads away to dodge the choking spray, until finally they would grab hold of one another and wrestle until the strongest one dunked his companion underwater, and then they would all disappear beneath the surface in a jumble of pale arms and legs before emerging together, puffing, choking, laughing, and struggling to catch their breath all at once.

When they were completely worn out, they would rush out and stretch themselves across the dry, hot sand, lying there while burying themselves beneath it, and eventually dash back to the water to repeat the whole routine again. Eventually it dawned on them that their bare skin looked quite a bit like flesh-colored "tights"; so they scratched a circle in the sand and created a circus—featuring three clowns, since none of them was willing to give up this most prestigious role to the others.

Next they got their marbles and played "knucks" and "ringtaw" and "keeps" until that game became boring. Then Joe and Huck went for another swim, but Tom wouldn't join them because he discovered that when he had pulled off his pants, he had also knocked his string of rattlesnake rattles off his ankle, and he wondered how he had avoided getting cramps for so long without the protection of this magical charm. He wouldn't go swimming again until he had found it, and by that time the other boys were exhausted and ready to take a break. They slowly drifted apart, became melancholy, and started staring wistfully across the wide river toward where the village lay sleeping peacefully in the sunshine. Tom found himself writing "BECKY" in the sand with his big toe; he scratched it out and felt annoyed with himself for being so weak. But he wrote it again anyway; he couldn't stop himself. He erased it one more time and then removed himself from temptation by gathering the other boys together and joining them.

But Joe's mood had sunk so low it seemed almost impossible to lift. He felt so homesick that he could barely stand the pain of it. Tears were ready to spill at any moment. Huck felt gloomy as well. Tom was discouraged too, but he worked hard to hide it. He was keeping a secret that he wasn't ready to share yet, but if this rebellious gloom didn't break soon, he would have to reveal it. He spoke with an exaggerated display of cheerfulness:

"I bet pirates have been on this island before, boys. We'll explore it again. They've hidden treasures here somewhere. How would you feel about finding a decaying chest full of gold and silver—hey?"

But it sparked only mild interest, which quickly disappeared without any response. Tom attempted one or two other tempting offers, but those failed as well. It was disheartening work. Joe sat stirring up the sand with a stick and looking very dejected. Finally he said:

"Oh, boys, let's give it up. I want to go home. It's so lonesome."

"Oh no, Joe, you'll feel better soon," said Tom. "Just think about all the fishing we can do here."

"I don't care for fishing. I want to go home."

"But, Joe, there isn't another swimming spot like this anywhere."

"Swimming isn't any good. I don't seem to enjoy it, somehow, when there isn't anybody to tell me I can't go in. I'm planning to go home."

"Oh, darn! Baby! You want to see your mother, I suppose."

"Yes, I do want to see my mother—and you would too, if you had one. I'm not any more of a baby than you are." And Joe sniffled a little.

"Well, we'll let the crybaby go home to his mother, won't we, Huck? Poor thing—does he want to see his mother? And so he shall. You like it here, don't you, Huck? We'll stay, won't we?"

Huck said, "Y-e-s"—without any heart in it.

"I'll never speak to you again as long as I live," Joe said, standing up. "There!" He walked away in a sullen mood and started getting dressed.

"Who cares!" said Tom. "Nobody wants you to. Go on home and get laughed at. Oh, you're a real pirate. Huck and I aren't crybabies. We'll stay, won't we, Huck? Let him go if he wants to. I think we can get along without him, perhaps."

But Tom felt troubled anyway and became worried when he saw Joe continue getting dressed with such a grim attitude. It was also unsettling to watch Huck stare so longingly at Joe's preparations while maintaining such a threatening silence. Soon, without saying goodbye, Joe started walking through the water toward the Illinois shore. Tom's heart began to sink. He looked over at Huck. Huck couldn't stand that look and looked away. Then he said:

"I want to come along too, Tom. Things were already getting so lonely, and now they're going to be even worse. Let's go with them, Tom."

"I won't! You can all go, if you want to. I mean to stay."

"Tom, I should go."

"Well, go ahead—who's stopping you."

Huck started gathering his scattered clothes. He said:

"Tom, I wish you would come along too. Think it over for a moment. We'll wait for you once we reach the shore."

"Well, you'll be waiting a damn long time, that's all."

Huck walked away sadly, while Tom stood watching him go, feeling a powerful urge in his heart to swallow his pride and follow along. Tom hoped the boys would pause and wait, but they continued wading slowly forward. It suddenly struck Tom how quiet and lonely everything had become. He fought one last battle with his pride, then rushed after his friends, shouting:

"Wait! Wait! I want to tell you something!"

They soon stopped and turned around. When he reached them, he started revealing his secret, and they listened glumly until they finally understood what he was getting at, and then they let out a loud cheer of approval and said it was "wonderful!" They added that if he had told them from the beginning, they wouldn't have walked away. He gave them a reasonable excuse; but his true reason had been the worry that even the secret wouldn't keep them with him for very long, so he had planned to save it as a final way to win them over.

The boys returned cheerfully and threw themselves back into their games with enthusiasm, talking constantly about Tom's amazing plan and praising how clever it was. After enjoying a delicious meal of eggs and fish, Tom announced that he wanted to learn how to smoke. Joe immediately liked the idea and said he would want to try it as well. So Huck prepared pipes and packed them with tobacco. These beginners had never smoked anything before except cigars made from grapevine, which stung the tongue and weren't considered grown-up anyway.

Now they stretched out on their elbows and started to smoke, carefully and without much confidence. The smoke tasted awful, and they choked a little, but Tom said:

"Why, it's just as easy! If I had known this was all there was to it, I would have learned long ago."

"I would too," said Joe. "It's just nothing."

"You know, I've watched people smoking many times and thought to myself that I wish I could do that too, but I never believed I actually could," Tom said.

"That's just how I am, isn't it, Huck? You've heard me talk exactly like that—haven't you, Huck? I'll let Huck decide whether I have or not."

"Yes—lots of times," said Huck.

"Well, I have too," Tom said. "Oh, hundreds of times. Once down by the slaughterhouse. Don't you remember, Huck? Bob Tanner was there, and Johnny Miller, and Jeff Thatcher, when I said it. Don't you remember, Huck, about me saying that?"

"Yes, that's right," said Huck. "That was the day after I lost a white marble. No, it was the day before."

"There—I told you so," said Tom. "Huck remembers it."

"I think I could smoke this pipe all day," said Joe. "I don't feel sick."

"I don't either," Tom said. "I could smoke all day long. But I bet Jeff Thatcher couldn't do it."

"Jeff Thatcher! He'd collapse after just two puffs. Let him give it a shot just once. He'd find out!"

"I bet he would. And Johnny Miller—I wish I could see Johnny Miller tackle it once."

"Oh, yes I do!" said Joe. "I bet Johnny Miller couldn't handle this at all. Just one small drink would knock him out."

"'It really would, Joe. Hey—I wish the boys could see us now."

"So do I."

"Listen—boys, don't mention anything about this, and sometime when they're nearby, I'll walk up to you and say, 'Joe, do you have a pipe? I want to smoke.' And you'll respond, kind of casually, as if it's nothing special, you'll say, 'Yes, I have my old pipe, and another one too, but my tobacco isn't very good.' And I'll say, 'Oh, that's fine, as long as it's strong enough.' And then you'll pull out the pipes, and we'll light up just as calmly, and then just watch them stare!"

"Wow, that'll be great, Tom! I wish it was happening now!"

"I do too! And when we tell them we learned this while we were off pirating, won't they wish they had come along with us?"

"Oh, I don't think so! I bet they will!"

The conversation continued for a while, but soon it started to lose momentum and became choppy. The quiet moments grew longer, and their spitting increased dramatically. Every part of the inside of the boys' mouths turned into a gushing fountain; they could barely swallow the saliva pooling under their tongues quickly enough to keep from drowning in it. Small amounts still trickled down their throats despite their best efforts, and each time this happened, they gagged suddenly. Both boys now looked extremely pale and sick. Joe's pipe slipped from his weak fingers. Tom's pipe fell as well. Both were salivating heavily and both were swallowing frantically with all their strength. Joe said weakly:

"I've lost my knife. I think I should go and find it."

Tom said, his lips trembling and his voice faltering:

"I'll help you. You go over that way and I'll search around by the spring. No, you don't need to come, Huck—we can find it."

So Huck sat down again and waited for an hour. Then he felt lonely and went to look for his friends. They were far apart in the woods, both very pale and fast asleep. But something told him that if they had encountered any problems, they had resolved them.

They didn't talk much during supper that evening. Both men appeared humble and subdued, and when Huck got his pipe ready after the meal and started to prepare theirs as well, they declined, saying they weren't feeling very well—something they had eaten at dinner hadn't agreed with them.

Around midnight Joe woke up and called to the boys. There was a heavy, oppressive feeling in the air that seemed to warn of something coming. The boys huddled close together and moved toward the comforting warmth of the fire, even though the stagnant, dead heat of the still atmosphere was suffocating. They sat quietly, focused and waiting. The serious silence continued. Beyond the firelight, everything disappeared into complete darkness. Soon there came a flickering glow that briefly revealed the leaves and then disappeared. After a while another came, slightly stronger. Then another. Then a soft moan came whispering through the forest branches and the boys felt a brief breeze on their faces, and trembled with the thought that the Spirit of the Night had passed by. There was a pause. Now a strange flash turned night into day and revealed every single blade of grass, separate and clear, that grew around their feet. And it revealed three pale, frightened faces as well. A deep rumble of thunder went rolling and tumbling across the sky and faded into angry grumbling in the distance. A gust of cold air swept by, stirring all the leaves and scattering the light ashes around the fire. Another intense flash lit up the forest and an immediate crash followed that seemed to split the treetops directly above the boys' heads. They held onto each other in fear, in the thick darkness that followed. A few large raindrops began pattering down on the leaves.

"Hurry! Boys, get to the tent!" Tom shouted.

They scattered in different directions, stumbling over roots and tangled vines in the darkness, each boy running a separate way. A fierce wind roared through the trees, making everything whistle and sing as it passed. One blinding lightning flash followed another, accompanied by thunderclap after thunderclap of deafening sound. Now a soaking rain began pouring down, and the growing hurricane drove it across the ground in heavy sheets. The boys called out to one another, but the howling wind and booming thunder completely drowned out their voices. Eventually, though, one by one they managed to make their way back and found shelter under the tent, cold, frightened, and soaked to the skin; but having companions in their misery felt like something to be thankful for. They couldn't talk because the old sail was flapping so violently, even if the other sounds had given them a chance. The storm grew stronger and stronger, and soon the sail broke free from where it was tied down and went flying away in the wind. The boys grabbed each other's hands and ran, stumbling and getting bruised many times, to take shelter under a large oak tree that stood on the riverbank. Now the storm was at its most intense. Under the constant display of lightning that blazed across the sky, everything below appeared in sharp and clear detail: the swaying trees, the churning river white with foam, the flying spray of water droplets, the faint outlines of the tall cliffs on the far side, visible through the moving clouds and the slanting curtain of rain. Every so often some massive tree gave up the struggle and came crashing down through the smaller trees; and the relentless thunder now came in ear-splitting explosive bursts, sharp and piercing, and incredibly terrifying. The storm reached its peak in one incredible display that seemed ready to tear the island apart, burn it completely, flood it to the treetops, blow it away, and deafen every living thing on it, all at the exact same time. It was a dangerous night for young people without shelter to be caught outside.

But finally the storm ended, and the forces retreated with increasingly faint threats and rumblings, and calm returned once more. The boys walked back to their camp, quite shaken; however, they discovered there was still reason to be grateful, because the massive sycamore tree that had sheltered their sleeping area was now destroyed, struck down by lightning, and they hadn't been beneath it when the disaster occurred.

Everything in the camp was soaked, including the campfire; they were just careless boys, typical of their generation, and hadn't prepared for rain. This was cause for alarm, since they were drenched and cold. They complained loudly about their situation; but they soon found that the fire had burned so far underneath the large log it had been built against (where it curved upward and lifted off the ground), that about a hand's width of it had stayed dry; so they worked patiently until, using strips and bark collected from the undersides of protected logs, they managed to get the fire burning again. Then they stacked on large dead branches until they had a blazing furnace, and their spirits lifted once more. They dried their boiled ham and enjoyed a feast, and afterward they sat by the fire and embellished and celebrated their midnight adventure until morning, since there wasn't a dry place to sleep anywhere around.

As the sun began to creep in on the boys, sleepiness overcame them, and they walked out onto the sandbar and lay down to rest. Eventually they got burned by the heat and wearily started preparing breakfast. Following their meal they felt sluggish and stiff, and somewhat homesick again. Tom noticed these warning signs and began trying to lift the spirits of his fellow pirates as best he could. However, they showed no interest in marbles, circus games, swimming, or any other activities. He brought up their impressive secret, which managed to spark a bit of enthusiasm. While this mood lasted, he got them excited about a new plan. The idea was to stop being pirates temporarily and become Indians instead. This concept appealed to them, so before long they had stripped off their clothes and painted themselves with black mud from head to toe, creating zebra-like stripes—naturally, they were all chiefs—and then they charged through the forest to raid an English settlement.

Gradually they split into three enemy tribes and launched surprise attacks on each other with terrifying battle cries, slaughtering and scalping one another by the thousands. It was a bloody day. As a result, it was an extremely satisfying one.

They gathered at camp around dinnertime, hungry and cheerful; but then a problem emerged—enemy Indians couldn't share a meal together without first making peace, and this was simply impossible without smoking a peace pipe. There was no other method they had ever known. Two of the natives almost regretted they had stayed pirates. Nevertheless, there was no alternative; so with whatever appearance of good spirits they could manage, they requested the pipe and took their turn smoking it as it was passed around, following proper custom.

And look, they were delighted they had embraced this wild behavior, because they had accomplished something; they discovered that they could now smoke a bit without needing to search for a missing knife; they didn't get sick enough to feel seriously miserable. They weren't about to waste this promising opportunity through lack of effort. No, they practiced carefully, after dinner, with pretty good results, and so they enjoyed a triumphant evening. They felt more proud and happy about their new skill than they would have been if they had scalped and skinned the Six Nations. We will leave them to smoke and talk and boast, since we have no more need for them right now.

Chapter XVII

But there was no joy in the small town that same peaceful Saturday afternoon. The Harper family and Aunt Polly's household were dressing in mourning clothes, overwhelmed with deep sorrow and countless tears. An extraordinary silence had settled over the village, even though it was typically quiet enough under normal circumstances. The townspeople went about their business in a distracted manner and spoke very little, though they frequently let out heavy sighs. The Saturday break from school felt like a burden to the children. They showed no enthusiasm for their games and slowly abandoned them altogether.

In the afternoon Becky Thatcher found herself wandering around the empty schoolyard, feeling deeply sad. But she discovered nothing there to make her feel better. She spoke to herself:

"Oh, if only I could have one of those brass fireplace tool handles again! But I don't have anything left to remember him by." And she held back a small sob.

Soon she stopped and said to herself:

"It happened right here. Oh, if I could do it all over again, I would never say that—I wouldn't say it for anything in the world. But he's gone now; I'll never, never, never see him again."

This thought overwhelmed her, and she walked away with tears streaming down her face. Soon a whole group of boys and girls—friends of Tom and Joe—gathered nearby, standing by the fence and speaking in hushed, respectful voices about what Tom had done the last time they saw him, and what Joe had said about this or that little thing (which now seemed filled with terrible meaning, as they could clearly understand!)—and each person pointed to the exact place where the missing boys had stood at that moment, then added something like "and I was standing right here—exactly like I am now, and pretending you were him—I was that close—and he smiled just like this—and then I felt something come over me, something—frightening, you know—and I didn't realize what it meant at the time, of course, but now I understand!"

Then a dispute broke out over who had last seen the dead boys alive, and many people claimed that grim honor, presenting evidence that had been more or less altered by the witnesses. When it was finally determined who had actually seen the departed last and spoken the final words with them, those fortunate individuals took on a kind of sacred significance and were stared at with envy by everyone else. One unfortunate boy, who had no other claim to importance, said with clearly visible pride in his memory:

"Well, Tom Sawyer beat me up once."

But that attempt at glory failed. Most of the boys could make the same claim, which made the achievement far less special. The group wandered off, still sharing memories of the fallen heroes in hushed, reverent voices.

When Sunday school ended the next morning, the church bell began to toll rather than ring in its usual manner. It was an exceptionally quiet Sabbath, and the sorrowful sound seemed to match the contemplative stillness that had settled over the natural world. The townspeople started to arrive, pausing briefly in the entrance hall to speak in hushed tones about the tragic occurrence. However, inside the sanctuary there was no whispering; only the somber rustling of fabric as the women made their way to their seats broke the silence. No one could recall the small church ever being so crowded. At last there came a waiting pause, an anticipatory quiet, and then Aunt Polly walked in, with Sid and Mary behind her, followed by the Harper family, everyone dressed in deep black, and the entire congregation, including the elderly minister, stood respectfully and remained standing until the grieving family had taken their seats in the front pew. Another shared silence followed, interrupted occasionally by stifled weeping, and then the minister extended his arms and offered a prayer. A touching hymn was performed, and the scripture reading came next: "I am the Resurrection and the Life."

As the service continued, the clergyman painted such vivid portraits of the virtues, the charming qualities, and the exceptional potential of the lost boys that every person present, recognizing these descriptions, felt a sharp pain when remembering how they had stubbornly refused to see these traits before, and had instead consistently noticed only the mistakes and shortcomings in the poor children. The minister also shared many heartwarming stories from the lives of the deceased that demonstrated their kind, generous spirits, and the congregation could now clearly understand how admirable and touching those moments had been, recalling with sorrow that when they actually happened, they had appeared to be outright mischief that deserved punishment. The congregation grew increasingly emotional as the sorrowful story unfolded, until finally the entire gathering broke down and joined the grieving family members in a collective outpouring of heartbroken weeping, with even the preacher succumbing to his emotions and crying from the pulpit.

A soft sound came from the gallery, though no one paid attention to it; moments later the church door squeaked open; the minister lifted his tear-filled eyes from his handkerchief and froze in place! One pair of eyes, then another, followed the minister's gaze, and then nearly all at once the entire congregation stood up and stared as the three supposedly dead boys walked down the aisle, with Tom leading the way, Joe following behind him, and Huck, looking like a mess in his tattered clothes, shuffling bashfully at the back! They had been hiding in the empty gallery the whole time, listening to their own funeral service!

Aunt Polly, Mary, and the Harpers rushed to embrace their

returned loved ones, covering them with kisses and expressing overwhelming gratitude, while poor Huck stood embarrassed and uneasy, unsure of what to do or where to escape from all those unfriendly stares. He hesitated and began to slip away quietly, but Tom grabbed him and said:

"Aunt Polly, it isn't fair. Someone has to be glad to see Huck."

"And so they shall. I'm glad to see him, poor motherless thing!" And the loving care Aunt Polly showered upon him was the one thing that could make him feel even more uncomfortable than he already was.

Suddenly the minister shouted at the top of his voice: "Praise God from whom all blessings flow—sing!—and put your hearts in it!"

And they did. Old Hundred rose with a triumphant burst, and while it shook the rafters, Tom Sawyer the Pirate looked around at the envious young people surrounding him and admitted to himself that this was the proudest moment of his life.

As the "sold" congregation filed out, they said they would gladly risk being made fools of again just to hear Old Hundred performed like that one more time.

Tom received more slaps and kisses that day—depending on Aunt Polly's changing moods—than he had deserved in an entire year before; and he could barely tell which showed more gratitude to God and love for him.

Chapter XVIII

That was Tom's great secret—his plan to come back home with his fellow pirates and attend their own funerals. They had floated across to the Missouri shore on a log at dusk on Saturday, coming ashore five or six miles downstream from the village; they had spent the night sleeping in the woods at the town's edge until almost dawn, and had then snuck through back streets and alleyways before completing their rest in the church balcony among a jumble of broken benches.

At breakfast on Monday morning, Aunt Polly and Mary showed Tom a lot of love and paid close attention to what he needed. There was more conversation than usual. During their talk, Aunt Polly said:

"Well, I'm not saying it wasn't a clever prank, Tom, keeping everyone worried sick for almost a week so you boys could have your fun, but it's a shame you could be so heartless as to let me suffer like that. If you could float over on a log to attend your own funeral, you could have found a way to come over and give me some sign that you weren't dead, just that you had run away."

"Yes, you could have done that, Tom," said Mary; "and I believe you would if you had thought of it."

"Would you really, Tom?" Aunt Polly asked, her face brightening with hopeful longing. "Tell me honestly, would you have done it if you had thought of it?"

"I—well, I don't know. It would have spoiled everything."

"Tom, I hoped you loved me that much," said Aunt Polly, with a hurt tone that made the boy uncomfortable. "It would have meant something if you had cared enough to think of it, even if you didn't actually do it."

"Now, Aunt Polly, that's not harmful," Mary pleaded; "it's just Tom's impulsive nature—he's always in such a hurry that he never stops to think about anything."

"What a shame. Sid would have thought about it. And Sid would have come and done it too. Tom, someday you'll look back when it's too late and wish you had cared a little more about me when it wouldn't have cost you much at all."

"Now, auntie, you know I do care for you," said Tom.

"I'd understand it better if your actions actually showed it."

"I wish I had thought about it," said Tom, sounding regretful; "but I dreamed about you, at least. That counts for something, doesn't it?"

"It's not much—even a cat can do that—but it's better than nothing. What did you dream?"

"Why, Wednesday night I dreamed that you were sitting over there by the bed, and Sid was sitting by the woodbox, and Mary next to him."

"Well, that's exactly what we did. That's what we always do. I'm happy that your dreams could go to even that much effort for us."

"And I dreamed that Joe Harper's mother was here."

"Why, she was here! Did you dream any more?"

"Oh, lots. But it's so dim, now."

"Well, try to remember—can't you?"

"Somehow it seems to me that the wind—the wind blew the—the—"

"Try harder, Tom! The wind did blow something. Come!"

Tom pressed his fingers against his forehead for an anxious moment, then said:

"I've got it now! I've got it now! It blew out the candle!"

"Have mercy on us! Keep going, Tom—keep going!"

"And it seems to me that you said, 'Why, I believe that that door—'"

"Go on, Tom!"

"Just give me a second to think—just a second. Oh, right—you said you thought the door was open."

"As I'm sitting here, I did! Didn't I, Mary! Go on!"

"And then—and then—well I can't be sure, but it seems like you made Sid go and—and—"

"Well? Well? What did I make him do, Tom? What did I make him do?"

"You made him—you—Oh, you made him shut it."

"Well, for heaven's sake! I've never heard anything like that in my entire life! Don't tell me there's nothing to dreams anymore. Sereny Harper is going to hear about this within the hour. I'd love to see her explain this away with her nonsense about superstition. Continue, Tom!"

"Oh, everything is becoming as clear as daylight now. Then you said I wasn't bad, just mischievous and reckless, and no more responsible than—than—I think it was a young horse, or something like that."

"And that's exactly what happened! Well, my goodness! Continue, Tom!"

"And then you began to cry."

"So I did. So I did. Not the first time, either. And then—"

"Then Mrs. Harper started crying and said Joe was exactly the same way, and she wished she hadn't punished him for taking the cream when she had thrown it out herself—"

"Tom! The spirit was upon you! You were prophesying—that's what you were doing! Good heavens, go on, Tom!"

"Then Sid said—he said—"

"I don't think I said anything," said Sid.

"Yes you did, Sid," said Mary.

"Shut your mouths and let Tom continue! What did he say, Tom?"

"He said—I think he said he hoped I was better off wherever I had gone, but if I had been better sometimes—"

"There, do you hear that! Those were his exact words!"

"And you silenced him quickly."

"I swear I did! There must have been an angel there. There was an angel there, somewhere!"

"And Mrs. Harper told about Joe scaring her with a firecracker, and you told about Peter and the painkiller—"

"As sure as I'm alive!"

"And then there was a whole lot of talk about dragging the river for us, and about having the funeral Sunday, and then you and old Miss Harper hugged and cried, and she went."

"That's exactly how it happened! That's exactly how it happened, as sure as I'm sitting right here in these very tracks. Tom, you couldn't have told it better if you had seen it yourself! And then what? Keep going, Tom!"

"Then I thought you prayed for me—and I could see you and hear every word you said. And you went to bed, and I felt so sorry that I took a piece of sycamore bark and wrote on it, 'We aren't dead—we're just off being pirates,' and put it on the table by the candle; and then you looked so peaceful, lying there asleep, that I thought I went over and leaned down and kissed you on the lips."

"Did you, Tom, did you! I forgive you for everything because of that!" And she grabbed the boy in a tight hug that made him feel like the worst criminal imaginable.

"It was very kind, even though it was only a dream," Sid said quietly to himself.

"Be quiet, Sid! A person does exactly the same thing in a dream as they would do if they were awake. Here's a big Milum apple I've been saving for you, Tom, if you were ever found again—now go on to school. I'm grateful to the good God and Father of us all that I've got you back, who is patient and merciful to those who believe in Him and follow His word, though goodness knows I don't deserve it, but if only the deserving ones received His blessings and had His help to get them through the difficult times, there would be few enough who would smile here or ever enter into His rest when the long night comes. Go on Sid, Mary, Tom—get yourselves going—you've delayed me long enough."

The children headed off to school, and the elderly woman went to visit Mrs. Harper to overcome her practical nature with Tom's incredible dream. Sid was wise enough not to voice what he was thinking as he walked out of the house. His thought was: "Pretty unlikely—such a lengthy dream without a single error in it!"

What a hero Tom had become! He didn't skip and jump around anymore, but walked with a dignified swagger like a pirate who knew everyone was watching him. And they really were watching; he tried to act like he didn't notice the stares or hear the comments as he walked by, but they nourished him like food and drink. Younger boys followed behind him, as proud to be seen with him and accepted by him as if he were the drummer leading a parade or the elephant at the front of a circus coming to town. Boys his own age pretended they didn't know he had been gone at all, but they were burning with jealousy inside. They would have given anything to have his dark, sun-bronzed skin and his dazzling fame, and Tom wouldn't have traded either one for an entire circus.

At school the children showered him and Joe with so much attention, and their eyes expressed such passionate admiration, that the two heroes quickly became unbearably conceited. They started sharing their adventures with eager listeners—but they had only just begun; with imaginations like theirs providing endless material, this storytelling wasn't likely to stop anytime soon. And when they finally pulled out their pipes and strolled around casually smoking, they had reached the absolute peak of fame.

Tom decided he could be independent of Becky Thatcher now. Glory was enough. He would live for glory. Now that he was distinguished, maybe she would want to "make up." Well, let her—she would see that he could be just as indifferent as some other people. Soon she arrived. Tom pretended not to see her. He moved away and joined a group of boys and girls and began to talk. Before long he noticed that she was skipping cheerfully back and forth with a flushed face and sparkling eyes, pretending to be busy chasing schoolmates, and screaming with laughter when she caught someone; but he noticed that she always made her captures near him, and that she seemed to glance deliberately in his direction at such times, too. It satisfied all the spiteful vanity that was in him; and so, instead of winning him over, it only made him more conceited and made him work harder to avoid showing that he knew she was around. Soon she stopped fooling around, and moved uncertainly about, sighing once or twice and glancing secretly and longingly toward Tom. Then she noticed that now Tom was talking more specifically to Amy Lawrence than to anyone else. She felt a sharp pain and became disturbed and uneasy at once. She tried to go away, but her feet betrayed her, and carried her to the group instead. She said to a girl almost at Tom's elbow—with fake liveliness:

"Mary Austin! You naughty girl, why didn't you come to Sunday school?"

"I did come—didn't you see me?"

"Why, no! Did you? Where did you sit?"

"I was in Miss Peters' class, where I always go. I saw you."

"Did you? That's strange—I didn't see you there. I wanted to tell you about the picnic."

"Oh, that's great. Who's going to give it?"

"My mom's going to let me have one."

"Oh, great; I hope she'll let me come."

"Well, she will. The picnic's for me. She'll let anybody come that I want, and I want you."

"That's really wonderful. When will it happen?"

"Eventually. Perhaps during vacation."

"Oh, won't it be fun! Are you going to have all the girls and boys?"

"Yes, everyone who's my friend—or wants to be," and she stole a quick glance at Tom, but he kept talking to Amy Lawrence about the awful storm on the island, and how the lightning split the huge sycamore tree "into pieces" while he was "standing just three feet away from it."

"Oh, may I come?" said Grace Miller.

"Yes."

"And me?" said Sally Rogers.

"Yes."

"And me, too?" said Susy Harper. "And Joe?"

"Yes."

And so it continued, with excited clapping until everyone in the group had asked for invitations except Tom and Amy. Then Tom casually turned away, still talking, and walked off with Amy. Becky's lips began to quiver and tears welled up in her eyes; she concealed these emotions with forced cheerfulness and kept chattering, but the excitement had drained from the picnic, and from everything else too; she escaped as quickly as possible and found a place to hide where she had what girls call "a good cry." Afterward she sat there brooding, her pride wounded, until the bell rang. She perked up then, with a vengeful look in her eyes, and shook her braided pigtails and declared she knew exactly what she was going to do.

During recess, Tom kept flirting with Amy, feeling triumphantly pleased with himself. He also wandered around looking for Becky, hoping to hurt her feelings by showing off his performance with Amy. Finally, he spotted her, but his confidence instantly plummeted. She was sitting comfortably on a small bench behind the schoolhouse, looking at a picture book with Alfred Temple—they were so engrossed in what they were doing, with their heads bent so close together over the book, that they seemed completely unaware of everything else around them. Intense jealousy surged through Tom's body. He started hating himself for wasting the opportunity Becky had given him to make up with her. He called himself an idiot and every other harsh name he could come up with. He felt like crying from frustration. Amy chatted cheerfully as they walked together, since her heart was full of joy, but Tom had lost his ability to speak. He wasn't listening to what Amy was saying, and whenever she paused waiting for a response, he could only mumble an awkward agreement that was just as likely to be inappropriate as not. He kept wandering back to the area behind the schoolhouse, over and over again, to torture himself by watching the painful scene unfolding there. He couldn't stop himself. What drove him crazy was seeing, or thinking he saw, that Becky Thatcher never once seemed to realize he was even alive. But she did notice him; she knew she was winning their battle, and she was happy to watch him suffer the way she had suffered.

Amy's cheerful chatter became unbearable. Tom hinted at things he needed to take care of; tasks that had to be completed; and time was running out. But it was useless—the girl kept talking. Tom thought, "Oh, damn her, am I ever going to get away from her?" Finally he had to attend to those matters—and she said innocently that she would be "around" when school ended. And he hurried away, resenting her for it.

"Any other boy!" Tom thought, grinding his teeth. "Any boy in the entire town except that Saint Louis show-off who thinks he dresses so well and is upper class! Oh, fine, I beat you up the first day you ever came to this town, mister, and I'll beat you up again! You just wait until I catch you alone! I'll just grab you and—"

And he acted out beating up an imaginary boy—punching the air and kicking and clawing. "Oh, you do, do you? You yell 'enough,' do you? Now then, let that teach you!" And so the imaginary beating was completed to his satisfaction.

Tom ran home at noon. His conscience couldn't take any more of Amy's grateful joy, and his jealousy couldn't handle any more of the other pain. Becky went back to looking at pictures with Alfred, but as the minutes slowly passed and Tom didn't come to suffer, her victory started to fade and she lost interest; seriousness and distraction followed, and then sadness; two or three times she perked up her ears at footsteps, but it was false hope; Tom didn't come. Finally she became completely miserable and wished she hadn't taken it so far. When poor Alfred, seeing that he was losing her attention without knowing why, kept calling out: "Oh, here's a great one! look at this!" she finally lost her patience, and said, "Oh, don't bother me! I don't care about them!" and broke into tears, and stood up and walked away.

Alfred moved closer to her side and was about to offer comfort, but she said:

"Go away and leave me alone, can't you! I hate you!"

So the boy stopped, wondering what he might have done wrong—since she had said she would look at pictures all during lunch break—and she continued walking, crying. Then Alfred went thoughtfully into the empty schoolhouse. He felt humiliated and angry. He easily figured out the truth—the girl had simply used him as a way to take out her anger on Tom Sawyer. This realization didn't make him hate Tom any less. He wished there was some way to get that boy in trouble without putting himself at much risk. Tom's spelling book caught his attention. Here was his chance. He gratefully opened it to the afternoon lesson and poured ink all over the page.

Becky happened to glance through a window behind him at that exact moment and witnessed what he did, then continued walking without revealing herself. She began heading home, planning to find Tom and tell him what she had seen; Tom would be grateful and their problems would be resolved. However, before she had walked even halfway home, she changed her mind. The memory of how Tom had treated her when she was discussing her picnic came flooding back with burning intensity and filled her with shame. She decided to let him receive his whipping for the torn spelling book, and furthermore, to despise him forever.

Chapter XIX

Tom came home feeling gloomy, and the first words his aunt spoke to him made it clear that he had come to the wrong place for sympathy:

"Tom, I have a mind to skin you alive!"

"Auntie, what have I done?"

"Well, you've done enough. Here I go over to Serena Harper, acting like a complete fool, expecting I'm going to make her believe all that nonsense about that dream, when suddenly I discover she'd found out from Joe that you were over here and heard all the conversation we had that night. Tom, I don't know what's going to happen to a boy who will behave like that. It makes me feel so terrible to think you could let me go to Serena Harper and make such a fool of myself without saying a word."

This revealed a completely different side of the situation. Tom's clever scheme from that morning had previously struck him as an amusing prank and quite clever. Now it simply appeared petty and disgraceful. He lowered his head and found himself at a loss for words for a moment. Then he said:

"Auntie, I wish I hadn't done it—but I didn't think."

"Oh, child, you never think. You never consider anything except your own selfishness. You managed to think about coming all the way over here from Jackson's Island in the middle of the night just to mock our troubles, and you thought to deceive me with that lie about a dream; but you could never think to feel sorry for us and spare us from our grief."

"Aunt, I understand now that what I did was cruel, but I didn't intend to be cruel. I really didn't, I promise. And anyway, I didn't come over here that night to make fun of you."

"What did you come for, then?"

"It was to tell you not to worry about us, because we hadn't drowned."

"Tom, Tom, I would be the most grateful person in this world if I could believe you ever had such a good thought, but you know you never did—and I know it, Tom."

"I really did, auntie—I swear I'm telling the truth."

"Oh, Tom, don't lie—don't do it. It only makes things a hundred times worse."

"It's not a lie, aunt; it's the truth. I wanted to spare you from grief—that's the only reason I came."

"I'd give anything in the world to believe that—it would make up for so many wrongs, Tom. I'd almost be happy that you ran away and behaved so badly. But it doesn't make sense; because, why didn't you tell me, child?"

"Well, you see, when you started talking about the funeral, I became completely caught up in the idea of us coming and hiding in the church, and I just couldn't bring myself to ruin it. So I simply put the piece of bark back in my pocket and stayed quiet."

"What bark?"

"The piece of bark I had written on to tell you we'd gone pirating. I wish now that you had woken up when I kissed you—I really do, honestly."

The harsh expression on his aunt's face softened and a sudden warmth appeared in her eyes.

"Did you kiss me, Tom?"

"Why, yes, I did."

"Are you sure you did, Tom?"

"Yes, I did, auntie—absolutely certain."

"Why did you kiss me, Tom?"

"Because I loved you so much, and you were lying there moaning, and I felt so sorry for you."

The words rang true. The elderly woman couldn't conceal the quiver in her voice as she spoke:

"Kiss me again, Tom!—and get going to school now, and don't bother me anymore."

The moment he left, she rushed to a closet and pulled out the tattered remains of a jacket that Tom had worn during his pirating adventure. Then she paused, holding it in her hand, and said to herself:

"No, I don't dare. Poor boy, I think he's lied about it—but it's a wonderful, wonderful lie, there's so much comfort that comes from it. I hope the Lord—I know the Lord will forgive him, because it came from such a good heart when he told it. But I don't want to discover it's a lie. I won't look."

She put the jacket away and stood there thinking for a moment. Twice she reached out to grab the garment again, and twice she held herself back. Once more she tried, and this time she strengthened her resolve with the thought: "It's a good lie—it's a good lie—I won't let it upset me." So she searched the jacket pocket. A moment later she was reading Tom's piece of bark through streaming tears and saying: "I could forgive the boy now, even if he'd committed a million sins!"

Chapter XX

There was something about the way Aunt Polly kissed Tom that completely lifted his spirits and filled him with joy once more. He headed off to school and was fortunate enough to encounter Becky Thatcher at the beginning of Meadow Lane. His emotions always influenced how he acted. Without hesitating for even a second, he rushed over to her and said:

"I was really mean to you today, Becky, and I'm so sorry. I'll never, ever act like that again for as long as I live—please forgive me, won't you?"

The girl stopped and looked at him with scorn:

"I'd appreciate it if you'd mind your own business, Mr. Thomas Sawyer. I'll never speak to you again."

She tossed her head and walked away. Tom was so shocked that he couldn't even think clearly enough to say "Who cares, Miss Know-it-all?" until it was too late to say it. So he remained silent. But he was furious nonetheless. He wandered into the schoolyard wishing she were a boy, and picturing how he would beat her up if she were. He soon ran into her and made a cutting comment as he walked past. She threw one back at him, and their angry split was complete. It seemed to Becky, in her burning anger, that she could barely wait for school to begin, she was so eager to see Tom get whipped for the damaged spelling book. If she had entertained any remaining thought of revealing Alfred Temple's guilt, Tom's insulting remark had completely eliminated it.

Poor girl, she had no idea how quickly she was heading toward trouble herself. The teacher, Mr. Dobbins, had reached middle age with an unfulfilled dream. His greatest desire was to become a doctor, but poverty had determined that he would be nothing more than a village schoolmaster. Every day he pulled a mysterious book from his desk and became completely absorbed in it whenever no classes were in session. He kept that book locked away. Every child in school was dying to get a look at it, but the opportunity never arose. Each boy and girl had their own theory about what kind of book it was, but no two theories matched, and there was no way to discover the truth. Now, as Becky walked past the desk, which sat near the door, she saw that the key was still in the lock! It was a perfect opportunity. She looked around, realized she was alone, and the next moment she held the book in her hands. The title page—Professor Somebody's Anatomy—meant nothing to her, so she started flipping through the pages. She immediately came across a beautifully engraved and colored illustration—a human figure, completely naked. At that moment a shadow fell across the page and Tom Sawyer walked through the door and saw the picture. Becky grabbed at the book to shut it and had the terrible misfortune of tearing the illustrated page halfway down the middle. She shoved the book back into the desk, turned the key, and broke into tears of shame and frustration.

"Tom Sawyer, you are just as mean as you can be, to sneak up on a person and look at what they're looking at."

"How could I know you were looking at anything?"

"You should be ashamed of yourself, Tom Sawyer; you know you're going to tell on me, and oh, what am I going to do, what am I going to do! I'll get whipped, and I've never been whipped at school before."

Then she stamped her little foot and said:

"Go ahead and be as mean as you want! I know something that's going to happen. Just wait and you'll see! I hate you, I hate you, I hate you!"—and she stormed out of the house with a fresh burst of tears.

Tom stopped moving, feeling quite overwhelmed by this sudden attack. After a moment, he thought to himself:

"What a strange kind of fool a girl is! Never been punished in school! Come on! What's a punishment! That's just like a girl—they're so sensitive and cowardly. Well, of course I'm not going to tell old Dobbins about this little fool, because there are other ways of getting back at her that aren't so cruel; but what does it matter? Old Dobbins will ask who tore his book. Nobody will answer. Then he'll do exactly what he always does—ask one student and then another, and when he gets to the right girl he'll know it, without anyone telling him. Girls' faces always give them away. They don't have any courage. She'll get punished. Well, it's quite a difficult situation for Becky Thatcher, because there's no way out of it." Tom thought about the situation a moment longer, and then added: "All right, though; she'd like to see me in exactly such a predicament—let her worry about it!"

Tom joined the crowd of playful students outside. In a few moments the teacher arrived and school began. Tom didn't feel much interest in his studies. Every time he sneaked a look at the girls' side of the room, Becky's face bothered him. Taking everything into account, he didn't want to feel sorry for her, yet he could barely help himself from doing so. He couldn't work up any real excitement that deserved the name. Soon the spelling-book incident was discovered, and Tom's mind became completely occupied with his own problems for a while after that. Becky snapped out of her miserable daze and showed genuine interest in what was happening. She didn't think Tom could escape his trouble by denying that he had spilled the ink on the book himself, and she was correct. The denial only seemed to make things worse for Tom. Becky thought she would be happy about that, and she tried to convince herself that she was pleased, but she discovered she wasn't sure. When things reached their worst point, she felt an urge to stand up and tell on Alfred Temple, but she made an effort and forced herself to stay quiet—because, she told herself, "he'll definitely tell about me tearing the picture. I wouldn't say a word, not even to save his life!"

Tom received his punishment and returned to his seat without feeling particularly upset, since he thought it was quite possible that he had accidentally spilled the ink on the spelling book himself during some playful roughhousing—he had denied it simply for appearance's sake and because that was the expected thing to do, and had maintained his denial as a matter of principle.

A full hour passed by, with the teacher dozing in his chair while the classroom filled with the quiet buzz of students working. Eventually, Mr. Dobbins sat up straight, yawned, and unlocked his desk drawer to reach for his book, though he seemed uncertain whether to pull it out or leave it there. Most of the students looked up lazily, but two of them watched his every move with focused attention. Mr. Dobbins handled his book distractedly for a moment, then pulled it out and settled back in his chair to read! Tom quickly looked over at Becky. She had the same terrified, helpless expression he'd seen on a rabbit with a gun pointed at its head. In that instant, he completely forgot about their argument. Fast—he had to do something! Something immediate! But the urgency of the situation froze his ability to think clearly. Wait—he had an idea! He would rush over and grab the book, dash through the door, and escape. But his determination wavered for just a split second, and the opportunity slipped away—the teacher opened the book. If only Tom could have that missed chance back again! It was too late. There was nothing he could do to help Becky now, he realized. The next moment, the teacher turned to face the class. Every student's eyes dropped under his stare. There was something in his expression that filled even the innocent students with dread. Silence stretched on for what felt like ten seconds—the teacher was building up his anger. Then he spoke: "Who tore this book?"

There wasn't a single sound. You could have heard a pin drop. The silence stretched on; the master examined each face one by one, looking for any trace of guilt.

"Benjamin Rogers, did you tear this book?"

A denial. Another pause.

"Joseph Harper, did you?"

Another denial. Tom's anxiety increased more and more under the slow agony of these events. The teacher looked over the rows of boys—thought for a moment, then turned to the girls:

"Amy Lawrence?"

A shake of the head.

"Gracie Miller?"

The same sign.

"Susan Harper, did you do this?"

Another disappointment. The next girl was Becky Thatcher. Tom was shaking all over with excitement and a feeling that the situation was hopeless.

"Rebecca Thatcher" [Tom looked at her face—it was pale with fear]—"did you tear—no, look at me" [her hands lifted in a pleading gesture]— "did you tear this book?"

A thought flashed through Tom's mind like a bolt of lightning. He jumped to his feet and yelled, "I did it!"

The entire class looked on in bewilderment at this unbelievable act of foolishness. Tom paused for a moment to collect his scattered thoughts; and when he walked forward to receive his punishment, the amazement, thankfulness, and worship that radiated from poor Becky's eyes seemed like adequate payment for a hundred beatings. Motivated by the magnificence of what he had done, he endured without a single cry the most brutal whipping that even Mr. Dobbins had ever given out; and he also accepted with complete indifference the additional harsh punishment of being ordered to stay two hours after school ended—because he knew who would be waiting for him outside until his imprisonment was over, and wouldn't consider the long wait time wasted, either.

That night, Tom went to bed plotting revenge against Alfred Temple. Becky had confessed everything to him, filled with shame and regret, including her own betrayal. But even his desire for revenge soon gave way to more pleasant thoughts, and he finally drifted off to sleep with Becky's last words echoing softly in his mind.

"Tom, how could you be so noble!"

Chapter XXI

Vacation was getting closer. The schoolmaster, who was always strict, became even more harsh and demanding than usual because he wanted the school to look good on "Examination" day. His rod and paddle were rarely put away now—at least when it came to the younger students. Only the oldest boys and young women of eighteen and twenty avoided being beaten. Mr. Dobbins' beatings were quite forceful too; even though he wore a wig to cover his completely bald and shiny head, he was only middle-aged, and his muscles showed no signs of weakness. As the big day drew near, all his cruel tendencies came out; he seemed to enjoy punishing even the smallest mistakes. The result was that the younger boys spent their days living in fear and pain, and their nights planning revenge. They never missed a chance to cause trouble for their teacher. But he always stayed one step ahead. The punishment that came after every act of revenge was so thorough and overwhelming that the boys always ended up much worse off than before. Finally, they worked together and came up with a plan that seemed like it would bring them a spectacular victory. They brought the sign painter's boy into their group, explained their scheme, and asked for his help. He had his own reasons for being excited about this, since the master lived with his father's family and had given the boy plenty of reasons to hate him. The master's wife would be going to visit the countryside in a few days, so nothing would get in the way of their plan; the master always prepared for important events by getting quite drunk, and the sign painter's boy said that when the teacher had reached the right level of intoxication on Examination Evening, he would "handle things" while the man dozed in his chair; then he would wake him up at just the right moment and rush him off to school.

When the time finally came, the exciting event arrived. At eight in the evening, the schoolhouse was brightly lit and decorated with garlands and arrangements of leaves and flowers. The teacher sat in his large chair on a raised platform, with his blackboard positioned behind him. He appeared reasonably relaxed. Three rows of benches on each side and six rows in front of him were filled by the town's important figures and the students' parents. To his left, behind the rows of townspeople, stood a large temporary platform where the students who would participate in the evening's program were seated; rows of young boys, cleaned up and dressed so formally they looked uncomfortable; rows of awkward older boys; clusters of girls and young women wearing fine cotton and muslin dresses, clearly aware of their exposed arms, their grandmothers' old jewelry, their pieces of pink and blue ribbon, and the flowers in their hair. The remainder of the building was packed with students who were not performing.

The exercises started. A very small boy got up and bashfully recited, "You'd scarce expect one of my age to speak in public on the stage," and so on—moving with stiff, jerky gestures that looked like they came from a machine that wasn't working quite right. However, he made it through without incident, despite being terribly frightened, and received enthusiastic applause when he performed his rehearsed bow and stepped back.

A slightly embarrassed girl spoke with a lisp, reciting "Mary had a little lamb," and so on, performed a curtsy that inspired sympathy from the audience, received her well-deserved applause, and sat down with flushed cheeks and a happy expression.

Tom Sawyer stepped forward with arrogant confidence and launched into the famous "Give me liberty or give me death" speech, delivering it with dramatic intensity and wild hand gestures, but he faltered halfway through. Terrible stage fright overwhelmed him, his legs trembled beneath him, and he felt like he might suffocate. While he clearly had the audience's sympathy, their silence was even more crushing than their pity would have been. The teacher scowled, which sealed his complete failure. Tom struggled for a moment longer before retreating in total defeat. Someone made a feeble attempt to clap, but the applause quickly faded away.

"The Boy Stood on the Burning Deck" came next, along with "The Assyrian Came Down" and other dramatic recitation pieces. After that came reading exercises and a spelling competition. The small Latin class performed their recitations admirably. Now it was time for the evening's main event—original "compositions" written by the young ladies. One by one, each girl stepped forward to the front of the platform, cleared her throat, held up her manuscript (tied with delicate ribbon), and began to read with careful attention to "expression" and proper punctuation. The topics were identical to those that had been explored on similar occasions by their mothers before them, their grandmothers, and undoubtedly all their female ancestors stretching back to the Crusades. "Friendship" was one theme; "Memories of Other Days"; "Religion in History"; "Dream Land"; "The Advantages of Culture"; "Forms of Political Government Compared and Contrasted"; "Melancholy"; "Filial Love"; "Heart Longings," and so on.

A common characteristic in these writings was a carefully cultivated and cherished sadness; another was an extravagant and lavish outpouring of "elegant language"; yet another was a habit of forcing in particularly favored words and phrases until they were completely overused; and a distinctive quality that clearly identified and damaged them was the persistent and unbearable moral lesson that dragged its weakened tail at the conclusion of each and every piece. Regardless of what the topic might be, an exhausting attempt was made to twist it into some angle or another that the ethical and spiritual mind could observe with moral improvement. The obvious dishonesty of these moral lessons was not enough to achieve the elimination of this practice from the schools, and it is not enough today; it never will be enough while the world exists, perhaps. There is no school in all our country where the young women do not feel compelled to end their compositions with a moral lesson; and you will discover that the sermon of the most lighthearted and the least devout girl in the school is always the longest and the most ruthlessly sanctimonious. But enough of this. Plain truth is disagreeable.

Let's go back to the "Examination." The first essay that was read aloud had the title "Is this, then, Life?" Maybe the reader can handle an excerpt from it:

In everyday life, how wonderful are the feelings that fill a young person's heart when looking forward to some exciting celebration! The imagination works busily, painting beautiful pictures of happiness. In her dreams, the devoted follower of fashion sees herself surrounded by the party crowd, 'the observed of all observers.' Her elegant figure, dressed in white gowns, spins through the complex steps of the joyful dance; her eyes shine the brightest, her steps are the lightest in the cheerful gathering.

"In such delightful fantasies time passes quickly, and the eagerly awaited moment arrives for her entry into this heavenly world that she has dreamed about so vividly. How magical everything seems to her captivated eyes! Each new experience is more enchanting than the previous one. But eventually she discovers that underneath this beautiful surface, everything is meaningless, the compliments that once delighted her spirit now sound harsh and grating to her ears; the ballroom no longer holds any appeal; and with damaged health and a bitter heart, she turns away with the realization that worldly pleasures cannot fulfill the deep yearnings of the soul!"

And the pattern continued in this way. Throughout the reading, there was a murmur of approval that arose from time to time, along with whispered exclamations of "How sweet!" "How eloquent!" "So true!" and similar remarks, and after the event concluded with a particularly moving sermon, the applause was enthusiastic.

Then a thin, melancholy girl stood up, whose face had the "interesting" paleness that comes from pills and indigestion, and read a "poem." Two stanzas of it will suffice:

"A
MISSOURI MAIDEN'S FAREWELL
TO
ALABAMA"

"Alabama, goodbye! I love you dearly! But I must leave you for a while now! Yes, sad thoughts of you fill my heart with sorrow, and passionate memories crowd my mind! I have wandered through your flowering woods; I have roamed and studied near the Tallapoosa's waters; I have listened to the Tallassee's rushing floods, and courted the dawn's light along the Coosa's banks.

"Yet I feel no shame in carrying such a full heart, nor do I blush to look back with tearful eyes; I am not departing from some foreign land, nor am I leaving these sighs to strangers. I found welcome and home within this state, whose valleys I now leave—whose church spires quickly fade from my sight. Cold indeed would be my eyes, and heart, and head, when, dear Alabama! they turn cold toward you!"

There were very few people there who understood what "tête" meant, but the poem was still very satisfying.

Next, a young woman with dark skin, black eyes, and black hair stepped forward. She paused for a dramatic moment, put on a tragic expression, and began to read in a slow, serious tone:

A Vision

The night was dark and stormy. Not a single star flickered around the heavenly throne above; instead, the deep rumbling of heavy thunder continuously echoed in the air, while terrifying lightning danced angrily through the cloudy chambers of heaven, appearing to mock the power that the famous Franklin had wielded over its terror! Even the fierce winds emerged together from their mysterious dwellings and roared about as if trying to add to the wildness of the scene with their force.

At such a time, so dark and dreary, my spirit deeply longed for human sympathy; but instead,

'My dearest friend, my counsellor, my comforter and guide—
My joy in grief, my second bliss in joy,' came to my side.

She moved like one of those radiant creatures imagined in the sunlit paths of imagination's paradise by the romantic and youthful, a queen of beauty adorned only by her own extraordinary loveliness. Her step was so gentle that it made no sound at all, and except for the enchanting sensation created by her warm touch, like other subtle beauties, she would have slipped away unnoticed—unsought. A peculiar melancholy settled upon her face, like frozen tears on December's cloak, as she gestured toward the conflicting forces outside and asked me to observe the two figures before us.

This terrifying piece filled about ten pages of written text and concluded with a sermon so devastating to anyone who wasn't Presbyterian that it won first place. This work was regarded as the absolute best presentation of the entire evening. When the town's mayor presented the prize to its writer, he gave an enthusiastic speech declaring it was by far the most "eloquent" piece he had ever heard, and that even Daniel Webster himself would be proud of such writing.

It's worth noting, by the way, that the number of pieces where the word "beauteous" was overused, and human experience was described as "life's page," was typical for what you'd normally expect.

Now the teacher, feeling relaxed and almost cheerful, moved his chair to the side, turned his back to the audience, and started drawing a map of America on the blackboard for the geography class to practice with. However, his shaky hand made a mess of it, and quiet giggles spread throughout the room. He realized what was wrong and tried to fix it. He erased lines and redrew them, but this only made them look worse, and the giggling became more obvious. He focused all his attention on his work now, as if he was determined not to let the laughter defeat him. He could feel everyone's eyes watching him; he thought he was doing better, yet the giggling continued and clearly grew louder. And it had good reason to. There was an attic above, with an opening directly over his head, and through this opening came a cat, hanging by a string tied around her back legs. She had a cloth wrapped around her head and mouth to stop her from meowing. As she slowly came down, she curved upward and scratched at the string, then swung downward and clawed at the empty air. The giggling grew louder and louder—the cat was just six inches from the focused teacher's head—down, down, a bit lower, and she grabbed his wig with her frantic claws, held on tight, and was instantly pulled back up into the attic with her prize still in her grasp! And how brightly the light reflected off the teacher's bald head—because the sign painter's apprentice had covered it with gold paint!

That ended the meeting. The boys had gotten their revenge. Summer vacation had arrived.

[*] NOTE: The supposed "compositions" referenced in this chapter are taken word-for-word from a book called "Prose and Poetry, by a Western Lady"—but they follow the typical schoolgirl writing style so perfectly that they work much better than any artificial imitations could.

Chapter XXII

Tom joined the new order of Cadets of Temperance, drawn to the flashy nature of their uniforms and ceremonial dress. He promised to give up smoking, chewing tobacco, and swearing for as long as he stayed a member. Now he discovered something new—specifically, that promising not to do something is the most reliable way in the world to make a person want to go and do exactly that thing. Tom soon found himself plagued with a craving to drink and curse; this craving became so powerful that only the hope of getting a chance to show himself off in his red sash prevented him from quitting the organization. The Fourth of July was approaching; but he soon abandoned that idea—gave it up before he had endured his constraints for even forty-eight hours—and pinned his hopes on old Judge Frazer, justice of the peace, who seemed to be on his deathbed and would likely have a large public funeral, since he held such an important position. For three days Tom worried deeply about the Judge's health and eagerly sought news about it. Sometimes his expectations soared—so high that he would dare to take out his ceremonial outfit and rehearse in front of the mirror. But the Judge had a very frustrating habit of going up and down. Finally he was declared to be recovering—and then getting better. Tom was disappointed; and felt wronged, as well. He submitted his resignation immediately—and that very night the Judge took a turn for the worse and died. Tom decided that he would never trust a man like that again.

The funeral was impressive. The Cadets marched in a manner that would have made the deceased member green with envy. Tom was free again, though—and that meant something. He could drink and curse now—but he was surprised to discover he didn't want to. The mere fact that he was allowed to do these things removed his desire for them and stripped away their appeal.

Tom soon found himself surprised to discover that his eagerly anticipated vacation was starting to feel somewhat tedious and drag on.

He tried keeping a diary, but nothing occurred for three days, so he gave it up.

The first African American minstrel show ever came to town and created quite a stir. Tom and Joe Harper organized a group of performers and were thrilled for two days.

Even the Fourth of July was disappointing in its own way, since it poured rain, which meant there was no parade, and the most important person in the world (at least in Tom's mind), Mr. Benton, who was a real United States Senator, turned out to be a crushing letdown—he wasn't twenty-five feet tall, or even close to that height.

A circus came to town. The boys spent the next three days playing circus in tents they made from old rag carpets—charging three pins for boys and two for girls to get in—and then they gave up on the circus game.

A phrenologist and a mesmerist arrived—then departed again, leaving the village more boring and depressing than before.

There were a few mixed parties with boys and girls, but they were so rare and so wonderful that they only made the painful empty periods in between hurt even more.

Becky Thatcher had gone to her Constantinople home to spend vacation with her parents—so there wasn't a bright side to life anywhere.

The terrible secret of the murder was a constant source of suffering. It was like a cancer that would never go away, bringing endless pain.

Then the measles arrived.

For two long weeks, Tom remained confined as a prisoner, completely cut off from the world and everything happening around him. He was extremely sick and had no interest in anything at all. When he finally managed to get back on his feet and walked weakly into town, a sad transformation had taken place in everything and everyone. A religious "revival" had swept through, and everyone had "found religion"—not just the grown-ups, but even the boys and girls. Tom wandered around, desperately hoping to see just one wonderfully sinful face, but he met with disappointment at every turn. He discovered Joe Harper reading the Bible and sadly turned away from this disheartening sight. He looked for Ben Rogers and found him helping the poor while carrying a basket full of religious pamphlets. He tracked down Jim Hollis, who pointed out how blessed his recent bout with measles had been as a divine warning. Every boy he ran into added another heavy weight to his sadness, and when he finally rushed in desperation to seek comfort from Huckleberry Finn, only to be greeted with a quote from the Bible, his heart shattered completely. He crawled back home and into bed, understanding that he was the only person in the entire town who was damned, forever and ever.

That night, a tremendous storm struck with torrential rain, deafening thunder crashes, and brilliant flashes of lightning that lit up everything. He pulled the blankets over his head and lay there in terrified anticipation, waiting for his fate to unfold, because he was absolutely certain that this entire commotion was meant for him. He was convinced that he had pushed the patience of the heavenly powers beyond their breaking point, and this storm was their response. While it might have seemed like overkill to use a whole artillery unit to kill a tiny insect, he saw nothing strange about the idea that such an elaborate and costly thunderstorm had been created specifically to destroy a insignificant creature like himself.

Eventually the storm exhausted itself and faded away without achieving what it had set out to do. The boy's initial reaction was to feel thankful and change his ways. His next thought was to hold off—since there might not be any additional storms coming.

The following day the doctors returned; Tom had suffered a setback. The three weeks he remained bedridden this time felt like an eternity. When he finally ventured outside again, he could barely feel thankful for having recovered, remembering how isolated his situation was, how alone and abandoned he felt. He wandered aimlessly down the street and discovered Jim Hollis serving as judge in a children's court that was putting a cat on trial for murder, with her victim, a bird, present as evidence. He came across Joe Harper and Huck Finn in an alley eating a stolen melon. Poor boys! they—like Tom—had experienced a setback.

Chapter XXIII

Finally, the quiet town came alive with excitement—and intense excitement at that: the murder trial was about to begin in court. It immediately became the most captivating subject of conversation throughout the village. Tom couldn't escape from it. Every mention of the murder made his heart tremble, because his guilty conscience and anxieties nearly convinced him that these comments were being made within his earshot as "tests"; he couldn't understand how anyone might suspect he knew something about the murder, yet he still felt uneasy surrounded by all this chatter. It left him feeling cold and shaken constantly. He brought Huck to an isolated spot to speak with him privately. It would provide some comfort to speak freely for a moment; to share his heavy burden of worry with someone else who was suffering. Additionally, he wanted to make sure that Huck had kept their secret.

"Huck, have you ever told anybody about—that?"

"About what?"

"You know what."

"Oh—of course I haven't."

"Never a word?"

"Not a single word, I swear. What makes you ask?"

"Well, I was afraid."

"Listen, Tom Sawyer, we'd be dead within two days if anyone discovered that. You know it's true."

Tom felt more at ease. After a moment of silence:

"Huck, no one could make you tell, could they?"

"Get me to tell? Why, if I wanted that half-breed devil to drown me, they could get me to tell. There isn't any other way."

"Well, that's fine then. I think we're safe as long as we keep quiet. But let's make the promise again anyway. It's more certain that way."

"I agree."

So they made their oath once more with fearsome ceremonies.

"What are people talking about, Huck? I've heard quite a lot of it."

"Talk? Well, it's just Muff Potter, Muff Potter, Muff Potter all the time. It keeps me constantly sweating, so much that I want to hide somewhere."

"That's exactly how they act around me. I think he's done for. Don't you sometimes feel bad for him?"

"Almost always—almost always. He's worthless; but then he's never done anything to hurt anybody. Just fishes a little, to get money to get drunk on—and loafs around quite a bit; but lord, we all do that—at least most of us—preachers and such. But he's kind of good—he gave me half a fish, once, when there wasn't enough for two; and lots of times he's kind of stood by me when I was out of luck."

"Well, he's fixed kites for me, Huck, and tied hooks onto my fishing line. I wish we could get him out of there."

"Wow! We couldn't get him out, Tom. And besides, it wouldn't do any good; they'd catch him again."

"Yes—they would. But I hate hearing them criticize him so harshly when he never did—that."

"I do too, Tom. God, I hear them say he's the most vicious-looking criminal in this area, and they wonder why he was never hanged before."

"Yes, they talk like that all the time. I've heard them say that if he were to get free they would lynch him."

"And they'd do it, too."

The boys talked for a long time, but their conversation offered them little comfort. As evening approached, they found themselves lingering around the area near the small, isolated jail, perhaps with some vague hope that something might occur to resolve their troubles. However, nothing took place; it appeared that no angels or fairies cared about this unfortunate prisoner.

The boys did what they had done many times before—they went to the cell bars and gave Potter some tobacco and matches. He was housed on the ground floor and there were no guards present.

His appreciation for their presents had always made them feel guilty before—but this time it hurt even more deeply. They felt like complete cowards and traitors when Potter said:

"You've been really good to me, boys—better than anyone else in this town. And I don't forget it, I don't. Often I say to myself, I say, 'I used to fix all the boys' kites and things, and show them where the good fishing spots were, and help them however I could, and now they've all forgotten old Muff when he's in trouble; but Tom doesn't, and Huck doesn't—they don't forget him,' I say, 'and I don't forget them.' Well, boys, I did a terrible thing—drunk and crazy at the time—that's the only way I can explain it—and now I have to hang for it, and it's right. Right, and for the best, too, I think—hope so, anyway. Well, we won't talk about that. I don't want to make you feel bad; you've been good friends to me. But what I want to say is, don't you ever get drunk—then you won't ever end up here. Stand a little further west—so—that's it; it's a great comfort to see faces that are friendly when a person's in such a mess of trouble, and nobody comes here but you. Good friendly faces—good friendly faces. Climb up on each other's backs and let me touch them. That's it. Shake hands—yours will come through the bars, but mine are too big. Little hands, and weak—but they've helped Muff Potter a lot, and they'd help him more if they could."

Tom returned home feeling utterly dejected, and that night his sleep was plagued with nightmares. Over the following two days, he lingered around the courthouse, pulled by an almost overwhelming urge to enter, yet compelling himself to remain outside. Huck was experiencing the exact same struggle. The two boys deliberately kept their distance from one another. Each would wander off periodically, but the same grim attraction inevitably drew them back. Tom listened carefully whenever bystanders strolled out of the courtroom, but he consistently heard troubling updates—the evidence was tightening ever more mercilessly around poor Potter. By the close of the second day, the townspeople were saying that Injun Joe's testimony remained solid and unwavering, and that there wasn't the slightest doubt about what the jury's decision would be.

Tom stayed out late that night and climbed back into bed through the window. He was extremely excited. Hours passed before he finally fell asleep. The entire village gathered at the courthouse the next morning, as this was going to be the big day. Men and women were represented almost equally in the crowded audience. After waiting for a long time, the jury walked in and took their seats; soon after, Potter was brought in, looking pale and worn out, frightened and without hope, wearing chains and placed where everyone's curious eyes could stare at him; equally noticeable was Injun Joe, as emotionless as always. There was another pause, and then the judge entered and the sheriff announced the court was in session. The typical quiet conversations among the lawyers and shuffling of papers followed. These details and the delays that came with them created an atmosphere of anticipation that was both impressive and captivating.

Now a witness was called who testified that he had found Muff Potter washing himself in the creek early in the morning when the murder was discovered, and that Potter had immediately slipped away when he saw him. After additional questioning, the prosecutor said:

"Take the witness."

The prisoner looked up briefly, but lowered his gaze again when his own lawyer spoke:

"I have no questions to ask him."

The next witness testified to discovering the knife near the body. The prosecutor stated:

"Take the witness."

"I have no questions to ask him," Potter's lawyer replied.

A third witness testified that he had frequently seen the knife in Potter's possession.

"Take the witness."

Counsel for Potter chose not to question him. The faces in the audience started to show irritation. Was this lawyer planning to abandon his client's life without even trying?

Several witnesses testified about Potter's suspicious behavior when he was brought to the murder scene. They were permitted to step down from the witness stand without facing cross-examination.

Every detail of the harmful events that took place in the cemetery that morning, which everyone there remembered so clearly, was presented by reliable witnesses, but Potter's attorney didn't cross-examine any of them. The confusion and frustration in the courtroom showed itself through whispers and earned a warning from the judge. The prosecutor then said:

"Through the sworn testimony of citizens whose honest word cannot be doubted, we have proven this terrible crime beyond any possibility of doubt against the unfortunate defendant standing before this court. We conclude our case here."

A groan escaped from poor Potter, and he buried his face in his hands, gently rocking back and forth as a heavy silence filled the courtroom. Many men felt deeply moved, and the compassion of many women showed itself through their tears. The defense attorney stood up and said:

"Your honor, when we made our opening statements at the beginning of this trial, we indicated our intention to prove that our client committed this terrible act while under the influence of a mindless and uncontrollable madness caused by alcohol. We have changed our mind. We will not present that defense." [Then to the clerk:] "Call Thomas Sawyer!"

A confused amazement appeared on every face in the courtroom, including Potter's own. Every eye focused with curious interest on Tom as he stood up and walked to the witness stand. The boy looked frantic, since he was terrified.

"Thomas Sawyer, where were you on the seventeenth of June, around midnight?"

Tom looked at Injun Joe's cold, hard expression and found himself unable to speak. The crowd waited in complete silence, holding their breath, but the words simply wouldn't come out. After a short while, though, the boy regained some of his courage and managed to speak loudly enough for part of the room to hear:

"In the graveyard!"

"A little bit louder, please. Don't be afraid. You were—"

"In the graveyard."

A scornful smile flickered across Injun Joe's face.

"Were you anywhere near Horse Williams' grave?"

"Yes, sir."

"Speak up—just a little louder. How close were you?"

"Near as I am to you."

"Were you hidden, or not?"

"I was hidden."

"Where?"

"Behind the elm trees at the edge of the grave."

Injun Joe gave a barely noticeable flinch.

"Is anyone with you?"

"Yes, sir. I went there with—"

"Hold on—wait just a minute. Don't worry about telling us your companion's name. We'll bring him forward when the time is right. Did you take anything with you when you went there?"

Tom paused and appeared puzzled.

"Speak up, my boy—don't be shy. The truth is always respectable. What did you take there?"

"Only a—a—dead cat."

There was a wave of laughter, which the court quickly suppressed.

"We're going to create the skeleton of that cat. Now, young man, tell us everything that happened—tell it in your own words—don't leave anything out, and don't be afraid."

Tom started speaking—tentatively at first, but as he became more passionate about his story, his words came more and more smoothly; soon every other sound stopped except his voice; every eye focused on him; with open mouths and held breath the listeners were captivated by his words, losing track of time, completely absorbed in the horrifying appeal of the story. The tension of suppressed feelings reached its peak when the boy said:

"—and as the doctor swung the board around and Muff Potter fell, Injun Joe jumped with the knife and—"

Crash! Quick as lightning the halfbreed sprang for a window, tore his way through all opposers, and was gone!

Chapter XXIV

Tom became a shining hero once again—beloved by the elderly and envied by the youth. His name was even immortalized in print when the local newspaper celebrated his achievements. Some people believed he might become President someday, provided he managed to avoid the gallows.

As always, the unpredictable and irrational world embraced Muff Potter warmly and treated him with as much kindness as it had previously mistreated him. But this kind of behavior reflects well on the world's character; therefore, it wouldn't be right to criticize it for this.

Tom's days were filled with glory and triumph, but his nights became periods of terror. Injun Joe haunted all his dreams, always with menace in his eyes. Almost nothing could convince the boy to venture outside after dark. Poor Huck suffered from the same misery and fear, because Tom had revealed the entire story to the lawyer the night before the important trial day, and Huck was deeply worried that his involvement in the matter might be discovered, even though Injun Joe's escape had spared him from having to testify in court. The unfortunate boy had gotten the attorney to promise silence, but what good was that? Since Tom's troubled conscience had driven him to the lawyer's home at night and forced him to tell a frightening story that his lips had kept secret under the most solemn and terrifying of promises, Huck's trust in humanity was nearly destroyed.

Every day, Muff Potter's thankfulness made Tom happy that he had said something; but every night he wished he had kept his mouth shut.

Half the time Tom was terrified that Injun Joe would never be caught; the other half he was scared that he actually would be captured. He was certain he could never feel safe or breathe easily again until that man was dead and he had seen the body with his own eyes.

Rewards had been offered, the entire area had been searched thoroughly, but Injun Joe was nowhere to be found. One of those all-knowing and intimidating figures, a detective, arrived from St. Louis, poked around everywhere, shook his head knowingly, appeared wise, and achieved the kind of remarkable success that members of his profession typically accomplish. In other words, he "discovered a clue." However, you cannot execute a "clue" for murder, so after the detective finished his work and returned home, Tom felt just as unsafe as he had before.

The slow days passed by, and each one left behind a slightly reduced burden of worry.

Chapter XXV

There comes a moment in every properly raised boy's life when he feels an overwhelming urge to go somewhere and search for buried treasure. This longing suddenly struck Tom one day. He went out to find Joe Harper, but couldn't locate him. Then he looked for Ben Rogers, but he had gone fishing. Soon he came across Huck Finn the Red-Handed. Huck would do perfectly. Tom brought him to a secluded spot and shared his plan with him in secret. Huck was eager to participate. Huck was always ready to join any adventure that promised fun and didn't require any money, since he had far too much of the kind of time that doesn't pay. "Where should we dig?" Huck asked.

"Oh, just about anywhere."

"Why, is it hidden everywhere?"

"No, it definitely isn't. It's hidden in very specific places, Huck—sometimes on islands, sometimes in rotting chests buried under the tip of a branch from an old dead tree, right where the shadow falls at midnight; but usually under the floor in haunted houses."

"Who hides it?"

"Why, robbers, of course—who did you think? Sunday school superintendents?"

"I don't know. If it was mine I wouldn't hide it; I'd spend it and have a good time."

"I would too. But thieves don't operate that way. They always hide it and leave it there."

"Don't they come after it anymore?"

"No, they think they will, but they usually forget where the marks are, or they end up dying. Either way, the treasure stays buried for a long time and gets rusty; eventually someone discovers an old yellowed paper that explains how to locate the marks—a document that needs to be decoded for about a week because it's mostly symbols and hieroglyphics."

"Hyro—which?"

"Hieroglyphics—pictures and symbols, you know, that don't seem to mean anything."

"Do you have one of those papers, Tom?"

"No."

"Well then, how are you going to find the marks?"

"I don't want any marks. They always bury it under a haunted house or on an island, or under a dead tree that has one limb sticking out. Well, we've tried Jackson's Island a little, and we can try it again sometime; and there's the old haunted house up the Still-House branch, and there are lots of dead-limb trees—tons of them."

"Is it under all of them?"

"What are you saying! No!"

"Then how are you going to know which one to choose?"

"Go for all of them!"

"Why, Tom, it'll take all summer."

"Well, what about that? Suppose you discover a brass pot containing a hundred dollars, all rusty and gray, or a rotting chest filled with diamonds. How does that sound?"

Huck's eyes lit up.

"That's excellent. More than excellent enough for me. Just give me the hundred dollars and I don't want any diamonds."

"All right. But I bet you I'm not going to dismiss diamonds. Some of them are worth twenty dollars each—there aren't any, hardly, that aren't worth seventy-five cents or a dollar."

"No! Is that so?"

"Certainly—anybody will tell you so. Haven't you ever seen one, Huck?"

"Not as I remember."

"Oh, kings have plenty of them."

"Well, I don't know any kings, Tom."

"I don't think you do. But if you were to go to Europe you'd see a lot of them hopping around."

"Do they hop?"

"Hop? Are you kidding me? No way!"

"Well, what did you say they did that for?"

"Well, I just meant you'd see them—not jumping around, obviously—why would they need to jump?—but I mean you'd simply see them—spread out here and there, you know, in a general sort of way. Like that old hunchbacked Richard."

"Richard? What's his last name?"

"He didn't have any other name. Kings only have a given name."

"No?"

"But they don't."

"Well, if they like it, Tom, that's fine; but I don't want to be a king and have only a first name, like a slave. But tell me—where are you going to dig first?"

"Well, I don't know. Suppose we tackle that old dead-limb tree on the hill on the other side of Still-House branch?"

"I agree."

So they grabbed a broken pick and a shovel, and started their three-mile walk. They arrived sweaty and out of breath, and collapsed in the shade of a nearby elm tree to rest and have a smoke.

"I like this," said Tom.

"So do I."

"Tell me, Huck, if we discover a treasure here, what are you planning to do with your portion?"

"Well, I'll have pie and a glass of soda every day, and I'll go to every circus that comes to town. I bet I'll have a wonderful time."

"Well, aren't you going to save any of it?"

"Save it? What for?"

"Why, so I'll have something to live on later."

"Oh, that won't do any good. Dad would come back to this town someday and get his hands on it if I didn't hurry up, and I'm telling you he'd spend it all pretty fast. What are you going to do with yours, Tom?"

"I'm going to buy a new drum, and a real sword, and a red necktie and a bulldog puppy, and get married."

"Married!"

"That's it."

"Tom, you—why, you're not thinking straight."

"Wait—you'll see."

"Well, that's the most foolish thing you could do. Look at dad and my mother. Fight! They used to fight constantly. I remember it very clearly."

"That's nothing. The girl I'm going to marry won't fight."

"Tom, I think they're all the same. They'll all give someone a hard time. Now you should think about this for a while. I'm telling you, you really should. What's the girl's name?"

"It's not a woman at all—it's a girl."

"It's all the same, I think; some people say gal, some say girl—both are probably right. Anyway, what's her name, Tom?"

"I'll tell you sometime—not now."

"All right—that'll do. It's just that if you get married, I'll be lonelier than ever."

"No you won't. You'll come and live with me. Now get moving and we'll go dig."

They worked and sweated for thirty minutes. No result. They labored for another thirty minutes. Still no result. Huck said:

"Do they always bury it this deep?"

"Sometimes—not always. Not generally. I think we haven't found the right place."

So they picked a new location and started over. The work moved slowly, but they were still making headway. They continued digging quietly for a while. Eventually Huck rested against his shovel, wiped the sweat from his forehead with his sleeve, and said:

"Where are you going to dig next, after we finish this one?"

"I think we should probably deal with that old tree over there on Cardiff Hill behind the widow's place."

"I think that will be a good one. But won't the widow take it away from us, Tom? It's on her land."

"She should take it away! Maybe she'd like to try it once. Whoever finds one of these hidden treasures, it belongs to them. It doesn't make any difference whose land it's on."

That was satisfactory. The work continued. After a while Huck said:

"Damn it, we must be in the wrong place again. What do you think?"

"It's really strange, Huck. I can't figure it out. Sometimes witches get involved. I think that might be what's causing the problem now."

"Darn! Witches don't have any power during the day."

"Well, that's true. I didn't think of that. Oh, I know what the problem is! What a bunch of fools we are! You have to find out where the shadow of the branch falls at midnight, and that's where you dig!"

"Well damn it, we've wasted all this work for nothing. Now this is just great, we have to come back at night. It's a really long way. Can you get out?"

"I'm sure I will. We have to do it tonight as well, because if anyone spots these holes they'll figure out immediately what's here and they'll go after it."

"Well, I'll come around and meow tonight."

"All right. Let's hide the tools in the bushes."

The boys arrived that night around the scheduled time. They sat in the shadows, waiting. It was an isolated spot, made solemn by ancient traditions. Spirits whispered through the rustling leaves, ghosts hid in the dark corners, the deep howling of a dog drifted up from the distance, and an owl responded with its haunting call. The boys felt subdued by these serious surroundings and spoke very little. Eventually they decided that midnight had arrived; they marked where the shadow fell and started digging. Their hopes began to grow. Their excitement increased, and their hard work matched their enthusiasm. The hole grew deeper and deeper, but each time their hearts leaped at the sound of the pick hitting something, they only faced fresh disappointment. It was just a rock or a piece of wood. Finally Tom said:

"It's no use, Huck, we're wrong again."

"Well, but we can't be wrong. We spotted the shadow exactly."

"I know it, but then there's another thing."

"What's that?"

"Well, we were just guessing back then. It was probably either too late or too early."

Huck dropped his shovel.

"That's it," he said. "That's exactly the problem. We have to give this up. We can never tell the right time, and besides, this kind of thing is too terrible, here at this time of night with witches and ghosts fluttering around like this. I feel like something's behind me all the time, and I'm afraid to turn around because maybe there are others in front waiting for a chance. I've been getting goosebumps all over ever since I got here."

"Well, I've been thinking the same thing, Huck. They almost always put a dead man there when they bury treasure under a tree, to guard it."

"Lordy!"

"Yes, they do. I've always heard that."

"Tom, I don't like to mess around much where there are dead people. A person's bound to get into trouble with them, for sure."

"I don't like to disturb them either. What if this one here decided to poke his head out and say something!"

"Don't Tom! It's awful."

"Well, it just is. Huck, I don't feel comfortable at all."

"Listen, Tom, let's abandon this place and try somewhere else."

"All right, I think we should."

"What'll it be?"

Tom thought for a moment, then said:

"The haunted house. That's it!"

"Darn it, I don't like haunted houses, Tom. They're a whole lot worse than dead people. Dead people might talk, maybe, but they don't come sliding around in a shroud when you're not paying attention, and peek over your shoulder all of a sudden and grind their teeth, the way a ghost does. I couldn't stand something like that, Tom—nobody could."

"Yes, but, Huck, ghosts don't just travel around at night. They won't stop us from digging there during the day."

"Well, that's true. But you know very well that people don't go near that haunted house during the day or at night."

"Well, that's mainly because they don't want to go anywhere a man has been killed—but nothing has ever been spotted around that house except at night—just some blue lights moving past the windows—no actual ghosts."

"Well, whenever you see one of those blue lights flickering around, Tom, you can be sure there's a ghost very close behind it. It makes perfect sense. Because you know that nobody but ghosts use them."

"Yes, that's true. But they don't come around during the day anyway, so what's the point of being afraid?"

"Well, all right. We'll tackle the haunted house if you say so—but I think it's taking chances."

They had begun walking down the hill by now. There in the center of the moonlit valley below them stood the haunted house, completely alone, its fences having disappeared long ago, thick weeds choking the very doorsteps, the chimney fallen into ruins, the window frames empty, one corner of the roof collapsed. The boys stared for a moment, half expecting to see a blue light dart across a window; then speaking in hushed voices, as was appropriate for the time and situation, they veered far to the right to give the haunted house plenty of space, and made their way home through the woods that decorated the back side of Cardiff Hill.

Chapter XXVI

Around noon the following day, the boys reached the dead tree where they had come to collect their tools. Tom was eager to head to the haunted house, and Huck felt much the same way—but then he suddenly spoke up:

"Listen here, Tom, do you know what day it is?"

Tom mentally went through the days of the week in his mind, and then quickly raised his eyes with a startled expression—

"Wow! I never once thought of that, Huck!"

"Well, I didn't either, but suddenly it occurred to me that it was Friday."

"Darn it, a person can't be too careful, Huck. We might have gotten into a terrible mess, taking on something like that on a Friday."

"Absolutely! You bet we would! There might be some lucky days, but Friday definitely isn't one of them."

"Anyone can figure that out. I don't think you were the first person to discover it, Huck."

"Well, I never said I was, did I? And Friday isn't everything, either. I had a terrible nightmare last night—I dreamed about rats."

"No! That's definitely a bad sign. Did they get into a fight?"

"No."

"Well, that's good, Huck. When they don't fight, it just means there's trouble brewing, you know. All we need to do is stay alert and keep out of it. We'll drop this for today and go play. Do you know Robin Hood, Huck?"

"No. Who's Robin Hood?"

"Why, he was one of the greatest men that was ever in England—and the best. He was a robber."

"Wow, I wish I was. Who did he rob?"

"Only sheriffs and bishops and wealthy people and kings, and others like them. But he never troubled the poor. He loved them. He always shared with them completely fairly."

"Well, he must have been a really good guy."

"I bet he was, Huck. Oh, he was the most noble man who ever lived. There aren't any men like that now, I can tell you. He could beat any man in England with one hand tied behind his back, and he could take his yew bow and hit a ten-cent piece every time from a mile and a half away."

"What's a yew bow?"

"I don't know. It's some kind of bow, obviously. And if he only hit that dime on the edge, he would sit down and cry—and swear. But we'll play Robin Hood—it's really fun. I'll teach you."

"I agree."

So they spent the entire afternoon playing Robin Hood, occasionally glancing longingly down at the haunted house and making comments about what tomorrow might bring and what possibilities awaited them there. As the sun started to set in the west, they headed home through the long shadows cast by the trees and were soon hidden from view in the forests of Cardiff Hill.

On Saturday, just after noon, the boys returned to the dead tree. They smoked and talked in the shade, then dug a bit more in their final hole, though not with much hope, but simply because Tom mentioned there were many instances where people had abandoned a treasure hunt after digging to within six inches of it, only to have someone else come along later and uncover it with a single shovel thrust. This attempt also failed, however, so the boys picked up their tools and left, feeling they hadn't gambled carelessly with luck, but had met all the proper requirements of treasure hunting.

When they arrived at the haunted house, there was something so strange and eerie about the complete silence that hung over the place under the scorching sun, and something so disheartening about how lonely and abandoned it appeared, that they hesitated for a moment, too frightened to go inside. Then they crept up to the door and took a nervous look. They saw a room overrun with weeds, no floor, bare walls without plaster, an old fireplace, empty windows, and a crumbling staircase; and scattered throughout were tattered and forgotten spider webs. They eventually went inside, moving quietly, their hearts beating faster, speaking in hushed tones, listening carefully for any sound, and keeping their muscles tight and ready to run at a moment's notice.

In a short time, getting used to the place reduced their fears and they examined it with a critical and interested eye, actually admiring their own courage while also being amazed by it. Then they decided they wanted to explore upstairs. This felt like cutting off their escape route, but they began challenging each other, and naturally there could only be one outcome—they tossed their tools into a corner and climbed up. Upstairs showed the same signs of deterioration. In one corner they discovered a closet that seemed to hold mystery, but that promise turned out to be false—it was completely empty. Their bravery was now strong and firmly under control. They were just about to head back down and start working when—

"Quiet!" said Tom.

"What is it?" whispered Huck, his face turning pale with fear.

"Shh!... There!... Do you hear it?"

"Yes!... Oh, my! Let's run!"

"Stay still! Don't move! They're heading straight for the door."

The boys lay flat on the floor, pressing their eyes against the gaps between the wooden boards, waiting in terrified agony.

"They've stopped.... No—they're coming.... Here they are. Don't whisper another word, Huck. My goodness, I wish I was out of this!"

Two men walked in. Each boy thought to himself: "There's that old deaf and mute Spanish man who's been around town once or twice recently—I've never seen the other man before."

The other man was a ragged, disheveled figure with an unpleasant face. The Spaniard wore a serape draped around him; thick white whiskers covered his face, long white hair flowed out from beneath his sombrero, and green goggles shielded his eyes. As they entered, the other man was speaking quietly; they settled on the ground facing the door with their backs against the wall, and the speaker kept talking. His demeanor grew more relaxed and his words became clearer as he continued:

"No," he said, "I've thought it all over, and I don't like it. It's dangerous."

"Dangerous!" growled the "deaf and mute" Spaniard—much to the boys' amazement. "Coward!"

This voice made the boys gasp and tremble with fear. It was Injun Joe's voice! There was silence for some time. Then Joe said:

"What's more dangerous than that job up there—but nothing's happened because of it."

"That's different. Way up the river like that, with no other houses around. It'll never be known that we tried, anyway, as long as we didn't succeed."

"Well, what could be more dangerous than coming here during the day! Anyone who saw us would be suspicious."

"I know that. But there wasn't any other place as convenient after that foolish job. I want to leave this shack. I wanted to yesterday, but it wasn't any use trying to get out of here, with those troublesome boys playing over there on the hill right in full view."

"Those troublesome boys" trembled once more under the influence of this comment, and reflected on how fortunate it was that they had recalled it was Friday and decided to postpone their plans by a day. Deep down, they wished they had waited an entire year.

The two men pulled out some food and prepared lunch. After a lengthy and contemplative silence, Injun Joe said:

"Listen here, kid—you need to go back up the river where you came from. Stay there until you hear from me. I'll take my chances sneaking into this town one more time to check things out. We'll pull off that risky job after I've looked around a bit and feel confident about our chances. Then we're heading to Texas! We'll make our escape together!"

This was satisfactory. Both men soon began yawning, and Injun Joe said:

"I'm exhausted and need to sleep! It's your turn to keep watch."

He crouched down among the weeds and quickly started snoring. His companion nudged him a couple of times, and he quieted down. Soon the lookout began to doze off; his head dropped lower and lower, and now both men were snoring.

The boys took a long, relieved breath. Tom whispered:

"Now's our chance—come!"

Huck said:

"I can't—I'd die if they woke up."

Tom pushed forward while Huck hesitated. Finally, Tom got up slowly and quietly, beginning to move by himself. However, the moment he took his first step, the unstable floor let out such a terrible creak that he collapsed, nearly paralyzed with fear. He didn't try a second time. The boys remained there, counting each slow-passing moment until it felt like time had stopped and forever was turning dull; then they felt relieved to see that the sun was finally going down.

Now one of the snoring sounds stopped. Injun Joe sat up and looked around—he smiled darkly at his companion, whose head had fallen forward onto his knees—kicked him gently with his foot and said:

"Here! You're a security guard, aren't you! All right, though—nothing's happened."

"Wow! Was I asleep?"

"Oh, sort of, sort of. It's almost time for us to get going, partner. What should we do with the little bit of loot we have left?"

"I don't know—leave it here like we always have, I suppose. There's no point in taking it away until we head south. Six hundred and fifty dollars in silver is quite a bit to carry around."

"Well—all right—it won't matter to come here once more."

"No—but I'd suggest coming at night like we used to—that would be better."

"Yes, but listen here; it might be quite a while before I get the right opportunity for that job; accidents could happen; it's not in such a great location; we'll just properly bury it—and bury it deep."

"Good idea," said the companion, who walked across the room, knelt down, lifted one of the back hearthstones and pulled out a bag that made a pleasant jingling sound. He took twenty or thirty dollars from it for himself and the same amount for Injun Joe, then handed the bag to the latter, who was now kneeling in the corner, digging with his bowie knife.

The boys instantly forgot all their fears and troubles. Their eyes gleamed with excitement as they watched every move. What incredible luck!—the magnificence of it was beyond anything they could have imagined! Six hundred dollars was enough money to make half a dozen boys wealthy! This was treasure hunting under the most favorable circumstances—there wouldn't be any troublesome uncertainty about where to dig. They kept nudging each other constantly—meaningful nudges that were easily understood, for they simply meant—"Oh, aren't you glad we're here now!"

Joe's knife hit something.

"Hello!" he said.

"What is it?" said his comrade.

"Half-rotted plank—no, it's a box, I think. Here—give me a hand and we'll see what it's doing here. Never mind, I've broken a hole."

He reached his hand inside and pulled it out—

"Man, it's money!"

The two men looked closely at the small collection of coins in their hands. The coins were made of gold. The boys watching from above felt just as thrilled and pleased as the men below.

Joe's friend said:

"We'll get this done quickly. There's an old rusty pickaxe over in the weeds in the corner on the other side of the fireplace—I spotted it just a moment ago."

He ran and fetched the boys' pick and shovel. Injun Joe grabbed the pick, examined it carefully, shook his head, mumbled something under his breath, and then started using it. The box was quickly dug up. It wasn't very big; it was reinforced with iron and had once been very sturdy before the passing years had damaged it. The men stared at the treasure for a while in happy silence.

"Partner, there are thousands of dollars here," said Injun Joe.

"It was always said that Murrel's gang used to be around here one summer," the stranger observed.

"I know it," said Injun Joe; "and this looks like it, I should say."

"Now you won't need to do that job."

The half-breed frowned. He said:

"You don't know me. At least you don't know everything about this situation. It's not just robbery—it's revenge!" and a cruel gleam blazed in his eyes. "I'm going to need your help with this. When we're done—then we head to Texas. Go back home to your Nance and your children, and wait until you hear from me."

"Well—if you say so; what should we do with this—bury it again?"

"Yes. [Ravishing delight overhead.] No! by the great Sachem, no! [Profound distress overhead.] I'd nearly forgotten. That pickaxe had fresh dirt on it! [The boys were sick with terror in a moment.] What's a pick and shovel doing here? What's the deal with fresh dirt on them? Who brought them here—and where did they go? Have you heard anyone?—seen anyone? What! bury it again and let them come and see the ground has been disturbed? Not exactly—not exactly. We'll take it to my hideout."

"Why, of course! I should have thought of that before. You mean Number One?"

"No—Number Two—under the cross. The other place is bad—too common."

"All right. It's nearly dark enough to start."

Injun Joe stood up and moved carefully from one window to another, peering outside with caution. After a moment he said:

"Who could have brought those tools here? Do you think they might be upstairs?"

The boys couldn't breathe. Injun Joe placed his hand on his knife, paused for a moment in uncertainty, then turned toward the stairway. The boys thought about the closet, but they had no strength left. The footsteps came creaking up the stairs—the unbearable terror of their situation awakened some desperate courage in the frightened boys—they were just about to dash for the closet when there was a crash of rotting wood and Injun Joe fell to the ground among the wreckage of the collapsed stairway. He picked himself up, swearing, and his companion said:

"What's the point of all that? If someone's up there, let them stay there—who cares? If they want to jump down now and get themselves into trouble, who's going to stop them? It'll be dark in fifteen minutes—and then they can follow us if they want to. I'm fine with that. In my opinion, whoever threw those things in here got a glimpse of us and thought we were ghosts or devils or something. I bet they're still running."

Joe complained for a while; then he agreed with his friend that whatever daylight remained should be used wisely to prepare for their departure. Soon after, they quietly left the house in the growing darkness and headed toward the river carrying their valuable box.

Tom and Huck stood up, feeling weak but enormously relieved, and watched them through the gaps between the house's logs. Follow them? Absolutely not. They were satisfied just to get back to solid ground without breaking their necks and head toward town over the hill. They didn't say much to each other. They were too busy despising themselves—despising the bad luck that led them to bring the shovel and pickaxe to that place. If not for that, Injun Joe would never have become suspicious. He would have buried the silver alongside the gold to wait there until his "revenge" was complete, and then he would have suffered the misfortune of discovering that money had gone missing. What cruel, cruel luck that those tools were ever taken there!

They decided to watch for that Spaniard when he came to town looking for opportunities to carry out his revenge, and follow him to "Number Two," wherever that place might be. Then a terrible thought struck Tom.

"Revenge? What if he's talking about us, Huck!"

"Oh, don't!" said Huck, nearly fainting.

They discussed the entire situation, and as they walked into town they decided to believe that he might actually be referring to someone else—or at the very least that he might only be talking about Tom, since Tom was the only one who had given testimony.

Very little comfort it gave Tom to face danger by himself! Having someone with him would definitely make things better, he thought.

Chapter XXVII

The day's adventure greatly troubled Tom's dreams that night. Four times he grasped that incredible treasure and four times it dissolved into nothing in his hands as sleep left him and consciousness returned him to the harsh reality of his disappointment. As he lay there in the early morning remembering the events of his amazing adventure, he realized they seemed strangely muted and distant—almost as if they had taken place in a different world, or in some long-ago time. Then it struck him that the great adventure itself must have been a dream! There was one very compelling reason supporting this theory—specifically, that the amount of money he had witnessed was too enormous to be genuine. He had never before seen as much as fifty dollars all together, and like all boys his age and background, he believed that all mentions of "hundreds" and "thousands" were simply imaginative ways of speaking, and that such amounts didn't actually exist in the real world. He had never once thought that such a large sum as a hundred dollars could be found in real money in anyone's possession. If his ideas about hidden treasure had been examined, they would have turned out to be made up of a handful of actual dimes and a pile of vague, magnificent, impossible-to-grasp dollars.

But the details of his adventure became noticeably sharper and clearer as he kept thinking them over, and soon he found himself starting to believe that it might not have been a dream after all. This uncertainty had to be cleared up. He would grab a quick breakfast and go find Huck.

Huck was sitting on the edge of a flatboat, lazily letting his feet hang in the water and looking very sad. Tom decided to let Huck bring up the topic first. If he didn't mention it, then the adventure would be proven to have been just a dream.

"Hello, Huck!"

"Hello, yourself."

Silence, for a minute.

"Tom, if we had left those tools at the dead tree, we would have gotten the money. Oh, isn't it terrible!"

"'It's not a dream, then, it's not a dream! Somehow I almost wish it was. I'll be damned if I don't, Huck."

"What isn't a dream?"

"Oh, that thing yesterday. I've been half thinking it was."

"Dream! If those stairs hadn't collapsed, you would have seen just how much of a dream it was! I've had enough dreams all night long—with that one-eyed Spanish devil coming after me throughout all of them—curse him!"

"No, don't destroy him. Find him! Follow the money trail!"

"Tom, we'll never find him. A guy only gets one chance at that kind of money—and we've lost it. I'd be pretty nervous if I actually saw him anyway."

"Well, I would too; but I'd still like to see him anyway—and follow him to his Number Two."

"Number Two—yes, that's it. I've been thinking about that. But I can't figure anything out from it. What do you think it is?"

"I don't know. It's too deep. Say, Huck—maybe it's the number of a house!"

"Great!... No, Tom, that's not it. If it is, it's not in this small town. There aren't any numbers here."

"Well, that's true. Let me think for a minute. Here—it's the number of a room—in a tavern, you know!"

"Oh, that's the trick! There aren't just two taverns. We can find out quickly."

"You stay here, Huck, until I return."

Tom left immediately. He didn't want Huck's company when he was out in public. He was gone for thirty minutes. He discovered that at the finest tavern, room number 2 had been rented by a young lawyer for quite some time and was still being used by him. At the more modest establishment, room number 2 remained a puzzle. The innkeeper's young son explained that the room stayed locked constantly, and he had never seen anyone enter or leave it except during nighttime hours; he couldn't think of any specific reason for this situation; he had felt some mild curiosity about it, but not very strongly; he had made the mystery more interesting by amusing himself with the thought that the room was "haunted"; he had observed that there had been a light glowing in there the previous night.

"That's what I've discovered, Huck. I think that's exactly the No. 2 we're looking for."

"I think it is, Tom. Now what are you going to do?"

"Let me think."

Tom thought for a long time. Then he said:

"I'll tell you. The back door of that Number 2 is the door that opens into that narrow alley between the tavern and the old run-down brick store. Now you collect all the door keys you can find, and I'll grab all of my aunt's keys, and on the first dark night we'll go there and test them. And remember, keep watching for Injun Joe, because he said he was going to come into town and look around once more for a chance to get his revenge. If you spot him, just follow him; and if he doesn't go to that Number 2, then that's not the right place."

"Lord, I don't want to follow him by myself!"

"Well, it will be nighttime, for sure. He might never even see you—and if he does, maybe he wouldn't think anything of it."

"Well, if it's pretty dark I think I'll follow him. I don't know—I don't know. I'll try."

"You can bet I'll follow him if it's dark, Huck. He might have discovered he couldn't get his revenge, and now he could be going straight after that money."

"That's right, Tom, that's exactly right. I'll follow him; I will, I swear!"

"Now you're talking! Don't you ever weaken, Huck, and I won't."

Chapter XXVIII

That night Tom and Huck were prepared for their adventure. They lurked around the tavern's vicinity until after nine o'clock, with one keeping watch on the alley from a distance while the other observed the tavern entrance. No one went into the alley or came out of it; no one who looked like the Spaniard went into or came out of the tavern door. The night appeared it would stay clear; therefore Tom headed home with the agreement that if significant darkness developed, Huck would come and make a cat call, at which point Tom would sneak out and test the keys. However, the night stayed bright, and Huck ended his surveillance and went to sleep in an empty sugar barrel around midnight.

Tuesday the boys had the same bad luck. Wednesday was no different. But Thursday night looked more promising. Tom snuck out early with his aunt's old tin lantern and a large towel to cover it with. He concealed the lantern in Huck's sugar barrel and they began their watch. An hour before midnight the tavern shut down and its lights (the only ones in the area) went out. No Spaniard had appeared. Nobody had gone into or come out of the alley. Everything seemed favorable. Complete darkness took over, and the total silence was broken only by the occasional rumbling of distant thunder.

Tom grabbed his lantern, lit it inside the barrel, wrapped it tightly in the towel, and both adventurers crept through the darkness toward the tavern. Huck remained on watch while Tom made his way into the alley. What followed was a period of anxious waiting that pressed down on Huck's mind like a heavy weight. He started wishing he could catch a glimpse of light from the lantern—it would scare him, but at least it would let him know that Tom was still alive. It felt like hours had passed since Tom had vanished. He must have surely passed out by now; perhaps he was dead; maybe his heart had given out from fear and excitement. Growing more restless, Huck found himself moving closer and closer to the alley, imagining all kinds of terrible possibilities and constantly expecting some disaster that would leave him breathless. There wasn't much breath to lose, since he could only manage to take in tiny gasps, and his heart would soon exhaust itself from beating so frantically. All at once there was a burst of light and Tom came rushing past him: "Run!" he shouted; "run for your life!"

He didn't need to say it twice; once was plenty; Huck was already moving at thirty or forty miles an hour before the words were repeated. The boys didn't stop running until they reached the shed of an abandoned slaughterhouse at the far end of town. Just as they made it inside for shelter, the storm broke and rain came pouring down. As soon as Tom caught his breath, he said:

"Huck, it was terrible! I tried two of the keys as quietly as I could, but they seemed to make so much noise that I could barely breathe I was so frightened. They wouldn't turn in the lock either. Well, without paying attention to what I was doing, I grabbed the doorknob, and the door swung open! It wasn't locked! I jumped inside and threw off the towel, and good heavens!"

"What! What did you see, Tom?"

"Huck, I almost stepped on Injun Joe's hand!"

"No!"

"Yes! He was lying there, fast asleep on the floor, with his old patch covering his eye and his arms stretched out wide."

"Oh my God, what did you do? Did he wake up?"

"No, he never moved. I think he was drunk. I just grabbed that towel and got started!"

"I never would have thought of the towel, I bet!"

"Well, I would. My aunt would make me really sick if I lost it."

"Hey, Tom, did you see that box?"

"Huck, I didn't wait to look around. I didn't see the box, I didn't see the cross. I didn't see anything but a bottle and a tin cup on the floor by Injun Joe; yes, I saw two barrels and lots more bottles in the room. Don't you see, now, what's the matter with that haunted room?"

"How?"

"Why, it's haunted with whiskey! Maybe all the Temperance Taverns have got a haunted room, hey, Huck?"

"Well, I suppose that might be true. Who would have thought such a thing? But listen, Tom, now's a really good time to get that box, if Injun Joe's drunk."

"That's exactly right! You give it a try!"

Huck shuddered.

"Well, no—I don't think so."

"And I don't think so, Huck. Just one bottle next to Injun Joe isn't enough. If there had been three bottles, he would be drunk enough and I'd do it."

There was a long pause for reflection, and then Tom said:

"Listen, Huck, let's not try that thing anymore until we know Injun Joe isn't in there. It's too frightening. Now, if we watch every night, we'll be absolutely certain to see him leave at some point, and then we'll grab that box faster than lightning."

"Alright, I agree. I'll keep watch all night long, and I'll do it every night as well, if you'll handle the other part of the work."

"Alright, I will. All you have to do is walk up Hooper Street for one block and meow—and if I'm sleeping, you can throw some gravel at the window and that will wake me up."

"Agreed, and good as wheat!"

"Now, Huck, the storm's over, and I'll go home. It'll begin to be daylight in a couple of hours. You go back and watch that long, will you?"

"I said I would, Tom, and I will. I'll haunt that tavern every night for a year! I'll sleep all day and I'll stand watch all night."

"That's all right. Now, where are you going to sleep?"

"In Ben Rogers' hayloft. He allows me to stay there, and so does his father's Black worker, Uncle Jake. I carry water for Uncle Jake whenever he needs me to, and anytime I ask him, he gives me a little something to eat if he can spare it. That's a really good man, Tom. He likes me because I never act like I'm better than him. Sometimes I've sat right down and eaten with him. But you don't need to tell anyone that. A person has to do things when they're terribly hungry that they wouldn't want to do all the time."

"Well, if I don't need you during the day, I'll let you sleep. I won't come around bothering you. Whenever you notice something's happening at night, just come right over and meow."

Chapter XXIX

The first thing Tom heard on Friday morning was wonderful news—Judge Thatcher's family had returned to town the previous evening. Both Injun Joe and the treasure suddenly became less important, and Becky became the center of the boy's attention. He met up with her and they had a wonderfully exhausting time playing "hispy" and "gully-keeper" with a group of their classmates. The day ended in an especially satisfying way: Becky convinced her mother to schedule the long-promised and repeatedly postponed picnic for the following day, and her mother agreed. The child's joy knew no bounds, and Tom's enthusiasm was equally intense. The invitations went out before sunset, and immediately all the young people in the village were caught up in excited preparation and eager anticipation. Tom's excitement kept him awake until quite late, and he had high hopes of hearing

Huck's "meow" signal and having treasure to amaze Becky and the other picnickers with the next day; but his hopes were dashed. No signal came that night.

Morning finally arrived, and by ten or eleven o'clock an excited and lively group had gathered at Judge Thatcher's house, with everything prepared for departure. It wasn't customary for older adults to spoil the picnics by attending. The children were thought to be safe enough under the supervision of a few young women around eighteen and several young men about twenty-three years old. The old steam ferry boat had been rented for the event; soon the cheerful crowd walked up the main street carrying baskets full of food. Sid was ill and had to miss the excitement; Mary stayed home to keep him company. The final thing Mrs. Thatcher said to Becky was:

"You won't get back until late. Perhaps you'd better stay all night with some of the girls that live near the ferry-landing, child."

"Then I'll stay with Susy Harper, mama."

"Very well. And mind yourself and behave properly and don't cause any trouble."

As they walked along together, Tom said to Becky:

"Listen—I'll tell you what we can do. Instead of going to Joe Harper's, we'll climb straight up the hill and stop at the Widow Douglas' place. She'll have ice cream! She has it almost every day—tons of it. And she'll be really happy to see us."

"Oh, that will be fun!"

Then Becky thought for a moment and said:

"But what will mama say?"

"How will she ever know?"

The girl considered the idea carefully and said with hesitation:

"I think it's wrong—but—"

"But come on! Your mother won't find out, so what's the problem? All she cares about is keeping you safe, and I'm sure she would have told you to go there if she had thought of it. I know she would!"

The Widow Douglas's wonderful hospitality was an irresistible temptation. Her invitation, combined with Tom's convincing arguments, quickly won out. They decided not to tell anyone about their plans for that night. Then Tom suddenly realized that Huck might show up this very evening and give the signal. This thought dampened his excitement considerably. Still, he couldn't bring himself to miss the fun at the Widow Douglas's house. And why should he give it up, he told himself—the signal hadn't come the night before, so why would it be any more likely to come tonight? The guaranteed enjoyment of the evening was more appealing than the uncertain treasure hunt; and, like any boy would, he chose to follow his stronger desire and refused to let himself think about the box of money for the rest of the day.

Three miles downstream from town, the ferryboat came to a stop at the entrance of a wooded valley and docked. The crowd poured onto the shore, and soon the distant forest and rocky peaks rang out everywhere with shouting and laughter. Every possible way to get overheated and exhausted was thoroughly explored, and eventually the adventurers wandered back to camp armed with hearty appetites, and then the feast began in earnest. Following the meal, there was a pleasant period of relaxation and conversation in the shade of the wide-spreading oak trees. After a while, someone called out:

"Who's ready for the cave?"

Everyone was excited. They gathered bundles of candles and immediately began scrambling up the hill. The cave's entrance was located on the hillside—an opening shaped like the letter A. Its heavy oak door stood open and unguarded. Inside was a small chamber, as cold as an icehouse, with walls formed by nature from solid limestone that glistened with cold moisture. Standing there in the deep darkness and looking out at the green valley gleaming in the sunlight felt romantic and mysterious. However, the impressive atmosphere quickly faded, and the playful chaos resumed. The instant someone lit a candle, everyone rushed toward the person holding it; a struggle and brave defense would follow, but the candle was soon knocked down or blown out, followed by joyful shouts of laughter and another chase. But everything must come to an end. Eventually, the group formed a line and made their way down the steep slope of the main passage, their flickering row of lights faintly illuminating the towering rock walls that nearly met sixty feet above their heads. This main passage was only eight to ten feet wide. Every few steps, other tall and even narrower cracks branched off from it on both sides—because McDougal's cave was nothing more than an enormous maze of winding corridors that connected to each other and separated again, leading nowhere in particular. People said that someone could wander for days and nights through its complex network of cracks and chasms without ever finding the cave's end; and that a person could go down, and down, and continue going down into the earth, encountering the same thing—maze beneath maze, with no end to any of them. No one truly "knew" the cave. Such a thing was impossible. Most of the young men were familiar with a section of it, and it wasn't usual to venture much beyond this familiar area. Tom Sawyer knew the cave as well as anyone.

The procession traveled down the main passage for about three-quarters of a mile, and then groups and pairs started to break away into side passages, rush through the gloomy tunnels, and surprise one another at places where the tunnels reconnected. Groups could avoid each other for up to half an hour while still staying within the familiar territory.

Gradually, one group after another came wandering back to the cave entrance, breathing heavily, laughing loudly, covered from head to toe with candle wax drippings, smudged with clay, and completely thrilled with how well the day had gone. They were then surprised to discover that they hadn't been paying attention to the time and that evening was nearly upon them. The loud bell had been ringing for thirty minutes. Still, this kind of ending to the day's adventures felt romantic and therefore satisfying. When the ferry carrying its excited passengers moved out into the water, no one except the boat's captain gave a damn about the lost time.

Huck was already keeping watch when the ferryboat's lights went glimmering past the dock. He didn't hear any sound from the vessel, since the young passengers were as quiet and still as people usually are when they're nearly exhausted. He wondered what boat it was and why it didn't stop at the dock—but then he pushed it from his thoughts and focused on his task. The night was becoming cloudy and dark. Ten o'clock arrived, and the sound of carriages stopped, scattered lights started to go out, all the remaining pedestrians vanished, the town settled into sleep and left the small watcher alone with the quiet and the shadows. Eleven o'clock came, and the tavern lights were extinguished; darkness was everywhere now. Huck waited what felt like an endlessly long time, but nothing occurred. His confidence was fading. Was there any point? Was there really any point? Why not abandon it and go to bed?

A sound reached his ears. Instantly, he became completely alert. The alley door shut quietly. He rushed to the corner of the brick building. The next moment, two men passed right by him, and one appeared to be carrying something under his arm. That had to be the box! So they were planning to take the treasure away. Why bother calling Tom now? It would be pointless—the men would escape with the box and disappear forever. No, he would stay on their trail and follow them; he would rely on the darkness to keep him hidden from detection. Thinking this through, Huck stepped out and moved silently behind the men, like a cat, barefoot, keeping them just close enough ahead so they wouldn't vanish from sight.

They walked up the river street for three blocks, then turned left onto a cross street. They continued straight ahead until they reached the path leading up Cardiff Hill, which they took. They passed the old Welshman's house halfway up the hill without pausing and kept climbing upward. Good, Huck thought, they're going to bury it in the old quarry. But they didn't stop at the quarry. They continued on, up to the summit. They dove into the narrow path between the tall sumac bushes and immediately disappeared into the darkness. Huck moved closer and reduced the distance between them, since they wouldn't be able to see him now. He jogged along for a while, then slowed his pace, worried he was catching up too quickly. He moved forward a bit more, then stopped completely and listened. No sound at all—nothing except what seemed like the beating of his own heart. An owl's hoot echoed over the hill—an ominous sound! But no footsteps. Good heavens, was everything lost! He was about to sprint forward when a man cleared his throat less than four feet away from him! Huck's heart jumped into his throat, but he forced it back down. Then he stood there trembling as if a dozen fevers had seized him all at once, so weak that he thought he would surely collapse to the ground. He knew exactly where he was. He realized he was within five steps of the fence leading into Widow Douglas' property. Very well, he thought, let them bury it there—it won't be difficult to find.

Now there was a voice—a very quiet voice—Injun Joe's:

"Damn her, maybe she has company—there are lights on, even though it's this late."

"I can't see any."

This was the voice of that stranger—the stranger from the haunted house. A deadly chill shot through Huck's heart—so this was the "revenge" job! His first thought was to run away. Then he remembered that the Widow Douglas had been kind to him on more than one occasion, and perhaps these men were planning to kill her. He wished he had the courage to warn her, but he knew he didn't dare—they might come after him and catch him. All these thoughts and more raced through his mind in the brief moment between the stranger's comment and Injun Joe's next words—which were—

"Because the bush is blocking your path. Now—this way—now you can see, can't you?"

"Yes. Well, there are people there, I think. Better give it up."

"Give it up, and I'm just leaving this country forever! Give it up and maybe never have another chance. I tell you again, as I've told you before, I don't care for her money—you may have it. But her husband was harsh with me—many times he was harsh with me—and mainly he was the justice of the peace that threw me in jail for being a vagrant. And that's not all. It's not even a tiny fraction of it! He had me whipped!—whipped in front of the jail, like a slave!—with all the town watching! Whipped!—do you understand? He took advantage of me and died. But I'll make her pay for it."

"Oh, don't kill her! Don't do that!"

"Kill? Who mentioned anything about killing? I'd kill him if he were here, but not her. When you want revenge on a woman, you don't kill her—nonsense! You target her appearance. You slice her nostrils—you cut notches in her ears like you would a pig!"

"By God, that's—"

"Keep your opinion to yourself! It will be the safest thing for you. I'll tie her to the bed. If she bleeds to death, is that my responsibility? I won't shed a tear if she does. My friend, you'll assist me with this matter—for my sake—that's why you're here—I might not be able to manage it alone. If you hesitate, I'll kill you. Do you understand that? And if I'm forced to kill you, I'll kill her too—and then I figure nobody will ever know much about who carried out this deed."

"Well, if it has to be done, let's get started. The sooner the better—I'm trembling all over."

"Do it now? With other people around? Listen—I'll start getting suspicious of you before you know it. No—we'll wait until the lights go out—there's no rush."

Huck sensed that silence was about to fall—something even more terrifying than any amount of deadly conversation; so he held his breath and carefully stepped backward; he placed his foot cautiously and steadily, after balancing precariously on one leg and nearly falling over, first to one side and then to the other. He took another step back, with the same careful attention and the same dangers; then another and another, and—a branch cracked beneath his foot! He stopped breathing and listened intently. There was no sound—the quiet was complete. He felt incredibly grateful. Now he turned around where he stood, between the walls of sumac bushes—turning himself as carefully as if he were a ship—and then moved quickly but cautiously forward. When he came out at the quarry he felt safe, and so he lifted his quick feet and ran. Down, down he raced, until he reached the Welshman's house. He pounded on the door, and soon the heads of the old man and his two strong sons appeared at the windows.

"What's all the commotion over there? Who's making that noise? What do you want?"

"Let me in—quick! I'll tell everything."

"Why, who are you?"

"Huckleberry Finn—quick, let me in!"

"Huckleberry Finn, really! That's not a name that'll get you very far, I'd say! But let him come in, boys, and let's find out what the problem is."

"Please don't ever tell anyone I told you," were Huck's first words when he got inside. "Please don't—I'd be killed for sure—but the widow has been good to me sometimes, and I want to tell—I will tell if you promise you'll never say it was me."

"Good heavens, he's definitely got something to say, or he wouldn't be acting like this!" the old man declared; "speak up and no one here will ever tell anyone, boy."

Three minutes later, the old man and his sons, well armed, had climbed the hill and were just entering the sumac path on tiptoe with their weapons ready in their hands. Huck went no further with them. He concealed himself behind a large boulder and began listening intently. There was a drawn-out, tense silence, and then suddenly there was an eruption of gunfire and a shout.

Huck didn't wait to hear any details. He jumped up and raced down the hill as fast as he could run.

Chapter XXX

As the first hint of dawn broke on Sunday morning, Huck made his way up the hill and knocked softly at the old Welshman's door. The people inside were sleeping, but it was a light sleep that could be easily disturbed because of the thrilling events from the night before. A voice called out from a window:

"Who's there!"

Huck's frightened voice responded quietly:

"Please let me in! It's only Huck Finn!"

"It's a name that can open this door any time, day or night, young man!—and you'll always be welcome!"

These words sounded strange to the homeless boy's ears, yet they were the most pleasant he had ever heard. He couldn't remember anyone ever using that final word when speaking about him before. The door was quickly unlocked, and he stepped inside. Huck was offered a chair while the elderly man and his two tall sons quickly got dressed.

"Now, my boy, I hope you're really hungry, because breakfast will be ready as soon as the sun comes up, and we'll have a nice hot one too—don't worry about that! The boys and I were hoping you'd show up and stay here last night."

"I was terribly frightened," said Huck, "and I ran. I took off when the guns fired, and I didn't stop for three miles. I've come now because I wanted to know about it, you know; and I came before daylight because I didn't want to run into those devils, even if they were dead."

"Well, poor fellow, you certainly look like you've had a rough night—but there's a bed waiting for you once you've eaten breakfast. No, they're not dead, son—we're sorry enough about that. You see, we knew exactly where to find them from your description; so we crept along quietly until we got within fifteen feet of them—that sumac path was as dark as a cellar—and right then I felt a sneeze coming on. It was the worst kind of luck! I tried to hold it back, but it was no use—it had to come out, and it did! I was leading the way with my pistol ready, and when the sneeze started, those criminals began rustling around to get out of the path. I shouted, 'Fire, boys!' and shot at the spot where the rustling was coming from. The boys did the same. But those villains were gone in an instant, and we chased after them through the woods. I don't think we hit any of them. They each fired one shot as they ran, but their bullets whistled past us without causing any damage. As soon as we couldn't hear their footsteps anymore, we stopped chasing and went to alert the constables. They gathered a group together and went to guard the riverbank, and as soon as it gets light, the sheriff and his men are going to search through the woods. My boys will join them shortly. I wish we had some kind of description of those scoundrels—it would help tremendously. But you couldn't see what they looked like in the dark, could you, son?"

"Oh yes; I saw them downtown and followed them."

"Excellent! Tell me about them—describe them, my boy!"

"One's the old deaf and mute Spaniard who's been around here once or twice, and the other's a mean-looking, ragged—"

"That's enough, boy, we know these men! We came across them in the woods behind the widow's place one day, and they sneaked away. Go on, boys, and tell the sheriff—get your breakfast tomorrow morning!"

The Welshman's sons left immediately. As they were walking out of the room, Huck jumped up and shouted:

"Oh, please don't tell anybody it was me that told on them! Oh, please!"

"That's fine if you say so, Huck, but you should get the recognition for what you accomplished."

"Oh no, no! Please don't tell!"

When the young men had left, the old Welshman said:

"They won't tell—and I won't. But why don't you want it known?"

Huck refused to explain any further, only saying that he already knew too much about one of those men and wouldn't want the man to find out that he knew anything damaging about him for anything in the world—he would definitely be killed for knowing it.

The elderly man promised to keep it secret once again, and said:

"How did you end up following these guys, kid? Did they seem suspicious to you?"

Huck remained quiet as he carefully thought through his response. Then he said:

"Well, you see, I'm kind of a tough case—at least that's what everyone says, and I can't argue with it—and sometimes I can't sleep much because I'm thinking about it and trying to figure out a new way of doing things. That's what happened last night. I couldn't sleep, so I walked up the street around midnight, turning it all over in my mind, and when I reached that old run-down brick store next to the Temperance Tavern, I leaned back against the wall to think some more. Well, just then these two guys came sneaking along close to me, carrying something under their arm, and I figured they had stolen it. One was smoking, and the other wanted a light, so they stopped right in front of me and their cigars lit up their faces. I could see that the big one was the deaf and mute Spaniard, recognizable by his white whiskers and the patch over his eye, and the other one was a shabby, rough-looking character."

"Could you see the rags by the light of the cigars?"

This caught Huck off guard for a moment. Then he said:

"Well, I don't know—but somehow it feels like I did."

"Then they continued on, and you—"

"I followed them—yes. That's what I did. I wanted to see what they were up to—they were sneaking around. I tracked them to the widow's fence, and stood in the dark and heard the raggedly dressed one plead for the widow, and the Spaniard swear he'd ruin her appearance just as I told you and your two—"

"What! The deaf and mute man said all that!"

Huck had made another awful mistake! He was doing everything he could to prevent the old man from getting even the slightest clue about who the Spaniard might be, but his tongue seemed bent on causing him trouble no matter how hard he tried. He made multiple attempts to escape from his predicament, but the old man was watching him closely and he kept making one error after another. Soon the Welshman said:

"My boy, don't be afraid of me. I wouldn't hurt a hair on your head for anything in the world. No—I'd protect you—I'd protect you. This Spaniard isn't deaf and mute; you've revealed that without meaning to; you can't hide that now. You know something about that Spaniard that you want to keep secret. Now trust me—tell me what it is, and trust me—I won't betray you."

Huck gazed into the old man's sincere eyes for a moment, then leaned down and whispered in his ear:

""That's not a Spaniard—it's Injun Joe!""

The Welshman nearly leaped from his chair. A moment later he said:

"It's all clear enough now. When you mentioned cutting ears and slashing noses, I figured that was your own addition, because white men don't seek that kind of revenge. But a Native American! That's completely different."

During breakfast the conversation continued, and as they talked, the old man mentioned that the final task he and his sons had completed before retiring for the night was to take a lantern and inspect the stile and the surrounding area for any traces of blood. They discovered none, but they did find a large bundle of—

"Of what?"

If those words had been bolts of lightning, they couldn't have burst from Huck's pale lips with more shocking suddenness. His eyes were now wide open, staring, and he held his breath—waiting for the response. The Welshman jerked back—stared right back at him—three seconds—five seconds—ten—then answered:

"Of burglar's tools. Why, what's wrong with you?"

Huck collapsed back, breathing softly but deeply, feeling incredibly grateful beyond words. The Welshman looked at him seriously and with curiosity, then said:

"Yes, burglar's tools. That seems to put your mind at ease quite a bit. But what made you so startled? What were you afraid we might have discovered?"

Huck found himself in a tight spot—someone was staring at him expectantly—he would have given anything for something to base a believable answer on—nothing came to mind—the questioning gaze was pressing harder and harder—a meaningless response presented itself—there was no time to consider it, so he took a chance and spoke it—weakly:

"Sunday-school books, maybe."

Poor Huck was too upset to smile, but the old man laughed loudly and happily, shaking his entire body from head to toe, and finished by saying that a good laugh like that was worth money because it reduced medical expenses significantly. Then he added:

"Poor old fellow, you look pale and worn out—you're not well at all—no wonder you're a bit scattered and unsteady. But you'll get through this. Rest and sleep should help you recover completely, I hope."

Huck felt annoyed with himself for acting like such a fool and showing such obvious excitement, since he had already dismissed the idea that the package from the tavern contained the treasure after overhearing the conversation at the widow's fence. However, he had only assumed it wasn't the treasure—he hadn't been completely certain—so when someone mentioned a seized bundle, he couldn't control his reaction. Still, he was actually happy the whole thing had occurred, because now he was absolutely sure that package wasn't the one they were looking for, which put his mind completely at ease. Everything actually seemed to be working out perfectly now; the treasure had to still be hidden in room No. 2, the criminals would be caught and locked up that very day, and he and Tom would be able to grab the gold that night without any difficulty or worry about being interrupted.

Just as breakfast was finished, someone knocked at the door. Huck quickly looked for a place to hide, since he didn't want to be linked in any way to what had happened the night before. The Welshman let in several ladies and gentlemen, including the Widow Douglas, and saw that groups of townspeople were walking up the hill to look at the fence. The news had clearly gotten out. The Welshman had to tell his visitors what had happened during the night. The widow openly expressed her gratitude for being saved.

"Don't say anything about it, ma'am. There's someone else you owe more to than you do to me and my boys, perhaps, but he won't let me reveal his name. We wouldn't have been there if it weren't for him."

Of course this sparked such enormous curiosity that it nearly overshadowed the main issue—but the Welshman let it gnaw at his visitors from the inside, and through them spread to the entire town, because he wouldn't reveal his secret. After everything else had been discovered, the widow said:

"I fell asleep while reading in bed and slept right through all that commotion. Why didn't you come and wake me up?"

"We decided it wasn't worth it. Those men weren't likely to return—they didn't have any tools left to work with, and what would be the point of waking you up and frightening you to death? My three Black men stood guard at your house for the rest of the night. They've just returned."

More visitors arrived, and the story needed to be told and retold for several additional hours.

There was no Sunday school during the regular school break, but everyone arrived early at church. The exciting incident was thoroughly discussed by all. Word spread that no trace of the two criminals had been found yet. After the sermon ended, Judge Thatcher's wife walked up beside Mrs. Harper as she made her way down the aisle with the crowd and said:

"Is my Becky going to sleep all day? I just thought she would be completely exhausted."

"Your Becky?"

"Yes," with a surprised expression—"didn't she spend the night at your place?"

"Why, no."

Mrs. Thatcher's face went white, and she collapsed into a church pew just as Aunt Polly walked past, chatting energetically with a friend. Aunt Polly said:

"Good morning, Mrs. Thatcher. Good morning, Mrs. Harper. I have a boy who has gone missing. I believe my Tom spent the night at one of your houses last night. And now he's too scared to come to church. I need to have a talk with him."

Mrs. Thatcher weakly shook her head and became even paler than before.

"He didn't stay with us," said Mrs. Harper, starting to look uncomfortable. A clear sense of worry appeared on Aunt Polly's face.

"Joe Harper, have you seen my Tom this morning?"

"No'm."

"When did you see him last?"

Joe tried to remember, but wasn't certain he could provide an answer. The congregation had stopped filing out of the church. Murmurs spread through the crowd, and an ominous anxiety settled over every face. Parents urgently questioned their children, and the young teachers were asked as well. Everyone said they hadn't paid attention to whether Tom and Becky were aboard the ferry during the return journey; it had been dark, and nobody had thought to check if anyone was absent. Finally, one young man voiced his terrible suspicion that they were still trapped in the cave! Mrs. Thatcher fainted on the spot. Aunt Polly burst into tears and began wringing her hands in despair.

The alarm spread from person to person, from one group to another, from street to street, and within five minutes the bells were ringing frantically and the entire town was awake! The Cardiff Hill incident immediately became unimportant, the burglars were forgotten, horses were prepared for riding, small boats were crewed, the ferry was called into service, and before half an hour had passed since the terrible news broke, two hundred men were rushing down the main road and along the river toward the cave.

Throughout the entire afternoon, the village felt deserted and lifeless. Numerous women came to visit Aunt Polly and Mrs.

Thatcher, attempting to offer them comfort. They wept alongside them as well, which proved more meaningful than any spoken words. During the long, wearisome night, the entire town remained awake waiting for updates; however, when morning finally broke, the only message they received was, "Send more candles—and send food." Mrs. Thatcher had nearly lost her mind with worry; Aunt Polly was in a similar state. Judge Thatcher sent hopeful and encouraging messages from the cave, but these offered no genuine comfort.

The elderly Welshman returned home as dawn approached, covered in candle wax, smeared with mud, and nearly exhausted. He discovered Huck still lying in the bed that had been prepared for him, burning with fever and speaking incoherently. All the doctors were at the cave, so Widow Douglas arrived and took responsibility for caring for the sick boy. She promised to do everything she could for him because, regardless of whether he was virtuous, wicked, or somewhere in between, he belonged to the Lord, and anything that belonged to the Lord deserved proper care. The Welshman mentioned that Huck had some good qualities, and the widow replied:

"You can count on it. That's God's mark. He doesn't leave it off. He never does. He puts it somewhere on every creature that comes from his hands."

Early in the morning, groups of exhausted men began to drift back into the village, but the strongest residents kept searching. The only news they could gather was that remote parts of the cave that had never been explored before were being thoroughly examined; every corner and crack would be searched completely; wherever someone wandered through the maze of tunnels, lights could be seen moving back and forth in the distance, and shouts and gunshots sent their hollow echoes through the dark passages. In one spot, far from the area usually visited by tourists, the names "BECKY & TOM" had been discovered traced on the rocky wall with candle smoke, and nearby lay a grease-stained piece of ribbon. Mrs. Thatcher recognized the ribbon and wept over it. She said it was the last keepsake she would ever have of her child, and that no other memento could ever be as precious, because this one had been the last thing to leave her living body before the terrible death came. Some said that occasionally, in the cave, a distant speck of light would appear, and then a joyful shout would ring out and twenty men would rush down the echoing passage—but then crushing disappointment always followed; the children were not there; it was only a searcher's light.

Three terrible days and nights slowly passed with their endless hours, and the village fell into a state of hopeless despair. Nobody had the energy or motivation for anything. The accidental discovery that had just been made—that the owner of the Temperance Tavern was keeping alcohol on his property—barely stirred any public interest, even though this was an enormous revelation. During a moment of clarity, Huck weakly brought up the topic of taverns, and eventually asked—with a vague fear of hearing bad news—whether anything had been found at the Temperance Tavern since he had been sick.

"Yes," said the widow.

Huck bolted upright in bed, his eyes wide with alarm:

"What? What was it?"

"Alcohol!—and the place has been closed down. Lie down, child—what a shock you gave me!"

"Just tell me one thing—only one—please! Was it Tom Sawyer who found it?"

The widow broke down in tears. "Quiet, quiet, child, quiet! I've told you before, you shouldn't be talking. You are extremely, extremely ill!"

Then they had discovered nothing except alcohol; there would have been quite an uproar if they had found the gold instead. So the treasure was lost for good—lost for good! But why would she be weeping? It was strange that she would cry.

These thoughts slowly made their way through Huck's mind, and exhausted by the mental effort, he fell asleep. The widow said to herself:

"There—he's asleep, poor soul. If only Tom Sawyer could find it! What a shame that someone can't find Tom Sawyer! Ah, there aren't many people left now who have enough hope, or enough strength for that matter, to keep on searching."

Chapter XXXI

Now to return to Tom and Becky's part in the picnic. They walked along the dark passages with the rest of the group, visiting the well-known wonders of the cave—wonders given rather elaborate names, such as "The Drawing-Room," "The Cathedral," "Aladdin's Palace," and so on. Soon the hide-and-seek games began, and Tom and Becky joined in enthusiastically until the activity started to become somewhat tiring; then they wandered down a winding corridor holding their candles high and reading the tangled network of names, dates, addresses, and sayings that covered the rocky walls (written in candle smoke). Still moving along and chatting, they barely noticed that they were now in a section of the cave whose walls were not decorated with writing. They wrote their own names under a protruding ledge and continued on. Soon they came to a spot where a small stream of water, dripping over a rock shelf and carrying limestone deposits with it, had, over countless ages, created a delicate and ruffled waterfall formation in shining and lasting stone. Tom squeezed his small body behind it to light it up for Becky's enjoyment. He discovered that it concealed a kind of steep natural staircase that was surrounded by narrow walls, and immediately the desire to be an explorer took hold of him.

Becky answered his call, and they created a smoke mark to guide them later, then began their exploration. They twisted and turned through various paths, venturing deep into the hidden depths of the cave, made another mark, and split off to search for interesting discoveries to share with the world above. At one location they discovered a large cavern, from whose ceiling hung numerous gleaming stalactites as long and thick as a man's leg; they walked around the entire space, filled with wonder and amazement, and eventually left through one of the many passages that led into it. This soon brought them to an enchanting spring, whose basin was covered with a delicate pattern of sparkling crystals; it sat in the center of a cavern whose walls were held up by many unusual pillars that had formed when large stalactites and stalagmites joined together, created by the constant dripping of water over hundreds of years. Beneath the ceiling enormous clusters of bats had gathered together, thousands packed into each group; the lights bothered these creatures and they came swooping down by the hundreds, screeching and diving aggressively at the candles. Tom understood their behavior and knew how dangerous this kind of situation could be. He grabbed Becky's hand and rushed her into the first tunnel they could find; and just in time, because a bat knocked out Becky's light with its wing as she was leaving the cavern. The bats pursued the children for quite a distance; but the fleeing pair ducked into every new passage they encountered, and finally escaped from the dangerous creatures. Tom soon discovered an underground lake, which extended its murky length into the distance until its outline disappeared in the darkness. He wanted to explore its edges, but decided it would be better to sit down and rest for a while first. Now, for the first time, the profound silence of the place cast a chilling effect upon the children's mood. Becky said:

"Why, I didn't notice, but it seems like such a long time since I heard any of the others."

"Now that I think about it, Becky, we're way down below them—and I have no idea how far north, south, east, or in whatever direction we are from them. We wouldn't be able to hear them from here."

Becky became worried.

"I wonder how long we've been down here, Tom? We should probably head back."

"Yes, I think we should. Maybe we should."

"Can you find the way, Tom? It's all a confusing mess to me."

"I think I could find it—but then there are the bats. If they blow out our candles, we'll be in a terrible situation. Let's try a different route so we don't have to go through there."

"Well. But I hope we don't get lost. That would be terrible!" and the girl shivered at the thought of what horrible things might happen.

They began walking through a corridor and traveled down it quietly for a long distance, looking at each new passage they came across to see if anything about it seemed familiar, but everything looked unfamiliar. Whenever Tom stopped to examine their surroundings, Becky would study his expression hoping for some sign of encouragement, and he would respond with forced cheerfulness:

"Oh, it's all right. This isn't the one, but we'll come to it right away!"

But with each unsuccessful attempt, his hope diminished further, and soon he started turning down random side passages out of sheer desperation, hoping against hope to find the right one. He continued to insist everything was "all right," but such heavy dread weighed on his heart that his words had lost their conviction and sounded as though he had declared, "All is lost!" Becky pressed close to him, consumed by terror, struggling desperately to hold back her tears, but they kept flowing. Finally she spoke:

"Oh, Tom, forget about the bats, let's go back that way! We keep getting into worse and worse trouble."

"Listen!" he said.

Profound silence; silence so deep that even their breathing was noticeable in the quiet. Tom shouted. The call echoed down the empty corridors and faded into the distance with a faint sound that resembled a ripple of mocking laughter.

"Oh, please don't do that again, Tom, it's absolutely terrible," Becky said.

"It's terrible, but I'm getting better, Becky; they might hear us, you know," and he shouted again.

The word "might" was even more terrifying than the ghostly laughter, as it revealed their hope was dying. The children stood motionless and listened carefully, but heard nothing in response. Tom immediately turned around and retraced their steps, walking quickly. It wasn't long before his uncertain movements revealed another frightening truth to Becky—he had lost their way back!

"Oh, Tom, you didn't make any marks!"

"Becky, I was such an idiot! Such an idiot! I never thought we might want to come back! No—I can't find the way. Everything's all confused."

"Tom, Tom, we're lost! We're lost! We'll never be able to get out of this terrible place! Oh, why did we ever leave the others!"

She collapsed to the ground and broke into such intense sobbing that Tom became terrified she might die or lose her mind. He sat down beside her and wrapped his arms around her; she pressed her face against his chest, clinging to him desperately as she poured out her fears and hopeless regrets, while the distant echoes transformed everything into mocking laughter. Tom pleaded with her to find hope again, but she told him she couldn't. He began criticizing and condemning himself for bringing her into this terrible situation; this approach worked better. She promised she would try to hope once more and would get up to follow him wherever he led, as long as he stopped talking that way. After all, she pointed out, he wasn't any more at fault than she was.

So they continued moving forward—without direction—purely by chance—all they were capable of was movement, staying in motion. For a brief moment, hope appeared to return—not because there was any logical reason for it, but simply because hope naturally resurfaces when it hasn't been worn down by years and repeated disappointments.

Soon Tom took Becky's candle and blew it out. This conservation meant everything! No words were necessary. Becky understood, and her hope faded once more. She knew that Tom had a complete candle and three or four pieces in his pockets—yet he had to save what they had.

Gradually, exhaustion started to take hold; the children struggled to stay focused, because the thought of stopping was terrifying when time had become so valuable. Moving in some direction, any direction at all, represented at least some progress and could lead to something positive; but stopping meant welcoming death and making it easier for death to catch up with them.

Finally, Becky's weak legs could no longer support her. She collapsed to the ground. Tom sat down beside her to rest, and they spoke about home, their friends back there, their cozy beds, and most importantly, the sunlight! Becky began to cry, and Tom searched for ways to console her, but all his words of encouragement had become worn out from overuse and now felt like cruel jokes. Exhaustion weighed so heavily on Becky that she drifted off to sleep. Tom felt relieved. He sat watching her tired face and noticed how it became peaceful and relaxed as pleasant dreams took over; gradually, a smile appeared and settled on her features. Her calm expression brought some comfort and hope to his own troubled mind, and his thoughts drifted back to earlier times and hazy recollections. While he was lost in these reflections, Becky awakened with a light, cheerful laugh—but the sound died instantly on her lips, replaced by a moan of despair.

"Oh, how could I have slept! I wish I had never, ever woken up! No! No, I don't mean that, Tom! Don't look at me like that! I won't say it again."

"I'm glad you've slept, Becky; you'll feel rested, now, and we'll find the way out."

"We can try, Tom; but I've seen such a beautiful country in my dream. I think we are going there."

"Maybe not, maybe not. Cheer up, Becky, and let's keep trying."

They stood up and walked along together, holding hands and feeling hopeless. They tried to figure out how long they had been trapped in the cave, but all they could determine was that it felt like days and weeks had passed, though it was obvious this couldn't be true since their candles hadn't burned out yet. Much later—they couldn't say exactly how much time had gone by—Tom said they needed to move quietly and listen for the sound of dripping water because they had to find a spring. Soon they discovered one, and Tom announced it was time to rest once more. Both were exhausted beyond measure, yet Becky mentioned she believed she could walk a bit further. She was shocked to hear Tom disagree with her. She couldn't make sense of it. They sat down, and Tom secured his candle to the wall in front of them using some clay. Their minds began to wander; neither spoke for quite a while. Finally, Becky broke the silence:

"Tom, I'm so hungry!"

Tom pulled something from his pocket.

"Do you remember this?" he said.

Becky almost smiled.

"It's our wedding cake, Tom."

"Yes—I wish it was as big as a barrel, because it's all we have."

"I saved it from the picnic so we could dream on it, Tom, the same way adults do with wedding cake—but it'll be our—"

She left her sentence unfinished. Tom divided the cake and Becky ate with a hearty appetite, while Tom only picked at his portion. There was plenty of cold water to complete their meal. After a while, Becky suggested that they continue moving. Tom remained quiet for a moment. Then he said:

"Becky, can you handle it if I tell you something?"

Becky's face turned pale, but she believed she could do it.

"Well then, Becky, we have to stay here where there's water to drink. That small piece is our last candle!"

Becky broke down into tears and sobbing. Tom did everything he could to comfort her, but it didn't help much. Finally Becky said:

"Tom!"

"Well, Becky?"

"They'll miss us and search for us!"

"Yes, they will! Certainly they will!"

"Maybe they're hunting for us now, Tom."

"Well, I suppose they probably are. I hope they are."

"When would they miss us, Tom?"

"When they get back to the boat, I reckon."

"Tom, it might be dark by then—would they notice we hadn't come back?"

"I don't know. But anyway, your mother would miss you as soon as they got home."

The frightened expression on Becky's face snapped Tom back to reality, and he realized he had made a terrible mistake. Becky wasn't supposed to go home that night! The children fell silent and became lost in thought. Suddenly, a fresh wave of tears from Becky revealed to Tom that the same realization had hit her too—that Sunday morning might be half over before Mrs. Thatcher discovered that Becky wasn't at Mrs. Harper's house.

The children fixed their gaze on their small piece of candle and watched it melt away slowly and mercilessly; they saw the half inch of wick standing alone at the end; they watched the weak flame rise and fall, climb the thin column of smoke, pause at its peak for a moment, and then—the terror of complete darkness took over!

How much time passed before Becky slowly became aware that she was crying in Tom's arms, neither of them could say. All they knew was that after what felt like an endless period, both woke up from a deep, death-like sleep and faced their suffering again. Tom said it might be Sunday now—perhaps Monday. He tried to get Becky to speak, but her grief was too overwhelming, and all her hope had disappeared. Tom said they must have been missed by now, and surely people were looking for them. He would call out and maybe someone would hear him. He attempted this, but in the darkness the far-off echoes sounded so terrifying that he didn't try again.

The hours dragged by, and hunger returned to torment the prisoners once more. Some of Tom's portion of the cake remained; they split it between them and ate it. However, they felt even hungrier than before. The meager bit of food only sharpened their craving.

Soon Tom said:

"Shh! Did you hear that?"

Both of them held their breath and listened carefully. They heard a sound that resembled the faintest, distant shout. Tom immediately responded to it, and taking Becky's hand, began feeling his way down the corridor toward the sound. Soon he stopped to listen once more; the sound came again, and it seemed to be slightly closer this time.

"It's them!" Tom exclaimed. "They're coming! Come on, Becky—we're safe now!"

The prisoners felt an almost overwhelming surge of joy. However, their progress was slow because pitfalls appeared frequently throughout the area and required careful navigation. Soon they encountered one of these obstacles and were forced to halt. The depth was impossible to determine—it could have been three feet or a hundred feet deep, but either way, there was no way to get across it. Tom lay flat on his stomach and stretched his arm down as far as possible into the opening. He couldn't reach the bottom. They had no choice but to remain where they were and wait for the search party to find them. They strained their ears to listen; clearly the distant voices calling out were becoming fainter! After another moment or two, the sounds disappeared completely. The crushing despair of their situation settled over them! Tom shouted and called out until his voice became hoarse, but his efforts proved futile. He spoke encouraging words to Becky, trying to maintain hope; but what felt like an eternity of worried waiting went by without any sounds returning.

The children felt their way back to the spring. The exhausting time crawled by; they fell asleep again, and woke up starving and heartbroken. Tom thought it must be Tuesday by now.

Now an idea came to him. There were some side passages nearby. It would be better to explore some of these rather than endure the burden of the long hours doing nothing. He pulled a kite string from his pocket, tied it to a jutting rock, and he and Becky began moving forward, with Tom leading the way, letting out the string as he felt his way along. After twenty steps, the corridor came to an abrupt end at a "jumping-off place." Tom dropped to his knees and felt around below, then reached as far around the corner as his hands could comfortably go; he tried to stretch just a little farther to the right, and at that instant, less than twenty yards away, a human hand holding a candle emerged from behind a rock! Tom let out a joyful shout, and immediately that hand was followed by the body it belonged to—Injun Joe's! Tom froze completely; he couldn't move a muscle. He felt enormously relieved the next moment when he saw the "Spaniard" turn and run, disappearing from sight. Tom was puzzled that Joe hadn't recognized his voice and come over to kill him for his testimony in court. But the echoes must have changed how his voice sounded. Without question, that had to be it, he figured. Tom's terror weakened every muscle in his body. He told himself that if he had enough strength to make it back to the spring, he would remain there, and nothing would convince him to risk encountering Injun Joe again. He was careful not to let Becky know what he had actually seen. He told her he had simply shouted "for luck."

But hunger and misery eventually overcome fear. Another exhausting wait by the spring and another lengthy sleep brought new developments. The children woke up tormented by intense hunger. Tom figured it must be Wednesday or Thursday or maybe even Friday or Saturday by now, and that the search party had probably given up. He suggested exploring another tunnel. He felt ready to face Injun Joe and any other dangers. However, Becky was extremely weak. She had fallen into a gloomy state of indifference and couldn't be motivated. She said she would stay right where she was and wait to die—it wouldn't take long. She told Tom he could take the kite string and explore if he wanted to, but she begged him to return frequently to talk with her. She also made him promise that when the terrible moment arrived, he would remain beside her and hold her hand until everything was finished.

Tom kissed her, feeling his throat tighten with emotion, and pretended to be confident that he would find the search party or discover a way out of the cave; then he grabbed the kite string and crawled on his hands and knees down one of the tunnels, weakened by hunger and filled with dread about their fate.

Chapter XXXII

Tuesday afternoon arrived and gradually faded into twilight. The village of St. Petersburg remained in mourning. The missing children still hadn't been found. Public prayers had been said for them, along with countless private prayers offered with complete devotion, but no encouraging news emerged from the cave. Most of the search parties had abandoned their efforts and returned to their everyday routines, convinced that the children would never be discovered. Mrs. Thatcher had become seriously ill and spent much of her time in a delirious state. People found it heartbreaking to hear her calling out for her child, lifting her head to listen intently for a full minute, then wearily letting it fall back down with a groan. Aunt Polly had sunk into deep sadness, and her gray hair had turned almost completely white. The village settled in for the night on Tuesday, filled with sorrow and despair.

In the middle of the night, a wild ringing erupted from the village bells, and within moments the streets filled with frantic, half-dressed people who yelled, "Come out! Come out! They've been found! They've been found!" Tin pans and horns joined the noise, the townspeople gathered together and headed toward the river, where they met the children arriving in an open carriage pulled by cheering citizens, crowded around it, joined their journey home, and swept magnificently up the main street shouting cheer after cheer!

The village was lit up; no one went back to sleep; it was the most extraordinary night the small town had ever experienced. For the first thirty minutes, a stream of townspeople moved through Judge Thatcher's house, embracing the rescued children and kissing them, grasping Mrs. Thatcher's hand, attempting to speak but finding themselves unable to—and wandered out shedding tears everywhere.

Aunt Polly's happiness was complete, and Mrs. Thatcher's was almost there too. Her joy would be complete as soon as the messenger who had been sent with the incredible news to the cave delivered word to her husband. Tom was lying on a sofa with an excited audience gathered around him, telling the story of their amazing adventure. He added many dramatic details to make it even more exciting, and he finished by describing how he had left Becky behind and went off to explore on his own. He explained how he followed two passages as far as his kite string would allow him to go, then followed a third passage until the kite string was stretched to its absolute limit. He was just about to turn around and head back when he caught sight of a distant spot that looked like daylight. He dropped the string and felt his way toward it, pushed his head and shoulders through a small opening, and there he saw the mighty Mississippi River flowing past!

And if it had only been nighttime, he wouldn't have noticed that tiny spot of daylight and wouldn't have investigated that tunnel any further! He explained how he returned to get Becky and shared the exciting news, but she told him not to bother her with such nonsense because she was exhausted and knew she was going to die, and she wanted to. He described how he worked to persuade her and managed to convince her; and how she nearly died from joy when she had felt her way to where she could actually see the blue spot of daylight; how he squeezed his way out through the opening and then helped her get out; how they sat there and wept with happiness; how some men came by in a small boat and Tom called out to them and explained their situation and how starved they were; how the men didn't believe their incredible story at first, "because," they said, "you are five miles down the river below the valley where the cave is located"—then they brought them aboard, rowed to a house, fed them dinner, let them rest until two or three hours after dark, and then took them home.

Before sunrise, Judge Thatcher and the small group of searchers with him were located in the cave by following the string trails they had left behind them, and they were told the exciting news.

Three days and nights of exhausting work and starvation in the cave couldn't be recovered from immediately, as Tom and Becky quickly realized. They remained confined to their beds throughout Wednesday and Thursday, appearing increasingly exhausted and weakened as time passed. Tom managed to move around slightly on Thursday, ventured downtown on Friday, and was almost completely recovered by Saturday; however, Becky didn't emerge from her room until Sunday, and even then she appeared as though she had endured a debilitating sickness.

Tom found out that Huck was sick and visited him on Friday, but wasn't allowed into the bedroom; he couldn't get in on Saturday or Sunday either. After that, he was permitted to visit every day, but he was told to stay quiet about his adventure and not bring up any exciting subjects. The Widow Douglas remained nearby to make sure he followed these rules. When Tom got home, he heard about what had happened on Cardiff Hill; he also learned that the "ragged man's" body had finally been discovered in the river near the ferry dock; the man had probably drowned while attempting to get away.

About two weeks after Tom was rescued from the cave, he set out to visit Huck, who had become strong enough to handle exciting news, and Tom believed he had something that would fascinate him. Judge Thatcher's house was along Tom's route, so he stopped by to see Becky. The Judge and several friends encouraged Tom to tell his story, and someone sarcastically asked if he would want to return to the cave again. Tom replied that he thought he wouldn't mind doing so. The Judge said:

"Well, there are others just like you, Tom, I have no doubt about that. But we've taken care of that problem. Nobody will get lost in that cave anymore."

"Why?"

"Because I had its large door covered with boiler iron two weeks ago, and secured it with three locks—and I have the keys."

Tom's face went completely pale.

"What's wrong, boy! Here, run, someone! Get a glass of water!"

The water was brought and splashed onto Tom's face.

"Oh, now you're fine. What was wrong with you, Tom?"

"Oh, Judge, Injun Joe's in the cave!"

Chapter XXXIII

Within minutes, word had gotten around, and twelve boats filled with men were heading toward McDougal's cave, with the ferry following close behind, packed with passengers. Tom Sawyer rode in the boat that carried Judge Thatcher.

When they unlocked the cave door, a heartbreaking scene greeted them in the faint light of the cavern. Injun Joe lay sprawled on the ground, lifeless, his face pressed against the crack beneath the door, as though his desperate eyes had remained focused until his final breath on the sunlight and freedom of the world beyond. Tom felt deeply moved, understanding from his own ordeal just how much this unfortunate man had endured. Compassion stirred within him, yet at the same time he experienced an overwhelming sense of relief and safety that made him realize for the first time just how enormous a burden of fear had weighed on him ever since the day he had spoken out against this violent outlaw.

Injun Joe's bowie knife lay nearby, its blade broken in two pieces. The massive foundation beam of the door had been chipped and hacked through with painstaking effort; yet this labor was pointless, because the natural rock formed a ledge outside it, and against that unyielding material the knife had accomplished nothing; the only damage was to the knife itself. Even if there had been no rocky barrier, the work would still have been futile, because even if the beam had been completely cut through, Injun Joe could never have squeezed his body under the door, and he understood this. He had only carved at that spot to keep himself busy—to pass the endless time—to occupy his tormented mind. Usually, visitors would leave half a dozen candle stubs stuck in the cracks of this entrance area, but none remained now. The prisoner had found them all and eaten them. He had also managed to catch a few bats, and these too he had consumed, leaving only their claws behind. The poor wretch had starved to death. Nearby, a stalagmite had been slowly rising from the floor for countless ages, built up by water dripping from a stalactite above. The captive had broken off the stalagmite, and on the remaining stump he had placed a stone, carving out a shallow depression to catch the precious drop that fell once every three minutes with the monotonous regularity of a clock's ticking—a dessert spoonful every twenty-four hours. That drop had been falling when the Pyramids were new; when Troy fell; when the foundations of Rome were laid; when Christ was crucified; when the Conqueror created the British empire; when Columbus sailed; when the massacre at Lexington was "news."

It is falling now; it will continue falling long after all these events have faded into the distant past of history, into the dim memories of tradition, and have been consumed by the deep darkness of being forgotten. Does everything have a purpose and a mission? Did this drop fall patiently for five thousand years just to be ready for this brief human creature's need? And does it have another important task to complete ten thousand years from now? It doesn't matter. Many, many years have passed since the unfortunate half-breed carved out the stone to catch the precious drops, but even today the tourist gazes longest at that touching stone and that slowly dripping water when he comes to see the wonders of McDougal's cave. Injun Joe's cup ranks first among the cave's marvels; even "Aladdin's Palace" cannot compete with it.

Injun Joe was buried close to the cave entrance, and crowds of people came by boat and wagon from nearby towns and all the farms and small villages within seven miles of the area. They brought their children along with all kinds of food and supplies, and they admitted that they had enjoyed the funeral almost as much as they would have enjoyed watching an execution.

This funeral put an end to one particular development—the petition to the governor requesting Injun Joe's pardon. The petition had gathered numerous signatures; many emotional and passionate meetings had taken place, and a group of foolish women had been chosen to dress in deep mourning and cry before the governor, begging him to act mercifully and abandon his responsibilities. Injun Joe was thought to have murdered five residents of the town, but what did that matter? Even if he had been the devil himself, there would have been plenty of weak-minded people ready to sign their names to a pardon petition and shed tears over it from their constantly damaged and overflowing emotions.

The day after the funeral, Tom brought Huck to a secluded spot for a serious conversation. By now, Huck had heard the complete story of Tom's adventure from the Welshman and Widow Douglas, but Tom believed there was something they hadn't mentioned; this was what he wanted to discuss. Huck's expression grew somber. He said:

"I know what happened. You got into Number 2 and never found anything except whiskey. Nobody told me it was you, but I just knew it had to be you as soon as I heard about that whiskey business. And I knew you hadn't gotten the money because you would have contacted me somehow and told me, even if you kept quiet about it to everyone else. Tom, something has always told me we'd never get our hands on that treasure."

"Listen, Huck, I never said anything about that tavern owner. You know his tavern was perfectly fine on Saturday when I went to the picnic. Don't you remember you were supposed to keep watch there that night?"

"Oh yes! Why, it feels like about a year ago. It was that very night that I followed Injun Joe to the widow's."

"You followed him?"

"Yes—but you need to keep quiet about this. I think Injun Joe has left friends behind, and I don't want them turning against me and playing nasty tricks on me. If it weren't for me, he'd be down in Texas right now, safe and sound."

Then Huck shared his complete adventure in private with Tom, who had previously only heard about the Welshman's role in the story.

"Well," said Huck, eventually returning to the main issue, "whoever took the whiskey from Room 2 also took the money, I figure—either way, it's lost to us, Tom."

"Huck, that money was never in No. 2!"

"What!" Huck studied his friend's face carefully. "Tom, have you found a lead on that money again?"

"Huck, it's in the cave!"

Huck's eyes blazed.

"Say it again, Tom."

"The money's in the cave!"

"Tom—I'm being completely honest with you now—are you just having fun, or are you serious about this?"

"I'm serious, Huck—as serious as I've ever been in my life. Will you come in there with me and help me get it out?"

"I bet I will! I'll do it if we can find a clear path there without getting lost."

"Huck, we can do that without any trouble at all."

"Good as wheat! What makes you think the money's—"

"Huck, just wait until we get in there. If we don't find it, I'll agree to give you my drum and everything I've got in the world. I will, I swear."

"All right—it's fantastic. When do you say?"

"Right now, if you say it. Are you strong enough?"

"Is it far into the cave? I've been on my feet for a few days now, three or four days, but I can't walk more than a mile, Tom—at least I don't think I could."

"It's about five miles to get there the way anyone else would go, Huck, but there's a really short cut that only I know about. Huck, I'll take you right to it in a small boat. I'll float the boat down there, and I'll pull it back again all by myself. You won't have to lift a finger."

"Let's start right away, Tom."

"All right. We need some bread and meat, our pipes, and a small bag or two, plus two or three kite strings, and some of those newfangled things they call matches. I'm telling you, there were many times I wished I had some when I was in there before."

A little after noon, the boys borrowed a small boat from a local resident who wasn't around, and set off immediately. When they had traveled several miles downstream from "Cave Hollow," Tom said:

"Now you can see this cliff here looks exactly the same all the way down from the cave opening—no houses, no lumber yards, bushes all identical. But do you see that white spot up there where there's been a landslide? Well, that's one of my landmarks. We'll go ashore now."

They landed.

"Now, Huck, from where we're standing you could reach that hole I escaped from with a fishing pole. See if you can find it."

Huck searched everywhere around the area and found nothing. Tom proudly walked into a dense cluster of sumac bushes and said:

"Here you are! Look at it, Huck; it's the coziest hideout in this whole area. You need to keep quiet about it. I've always wanted to be a robber, but I knew I had to find a place like this, and figuring out where to find one was the problem. We've got it now, and we'll keep it secret, but we'll let Joe Harper and Ben Rogers join us—because obviously there has to be a Gang, or it wouldn't have any class. Tom Sawyer's Gang—that sounds amazing, doesn't it, Huck?"

"Well, it just does, Tom. And who are we going to rob?"

"Oh, just about anyone. Ambush people—that's usually how it's done."

"And kill them?"

"No, not always. Keep them in the cave until they pay a ransom."

"What's a ransom?"

"Money. You make them raise all they can from their friends; and after you've kept them a year, if it isn't raised then you kill them. That's the general way. Only you don't kill the women. You shut up the women, but you don't kill them. They're always beautiful and rich, and terribly scared. You take their watches and things, but you always take your hat off and talk politely. There isn't anybody as polite as robbers—you'll see that in any book. Well, the women get to loving you, and after they've been in the cave a week or two weeks they stop crying and after that you couldn't get them to leave. If you drove them out they'd turn right around and come back. It's so in all the books."

"Wow, this is really great, Tom. I think it's even better than being a pirate."

"Yes, it's better in some ways, because it's close to home and circuses and all that."

By this time everything was prepared and the boys went into the hole, with Tom leading the way. They worked their way through to the far end of the tunnel, then secured their joined kite strings and continued forward. A few steps brought them to the spring, and Tom felt a tremor run through his entire body. He pointed out to Huck the piece of candle wick sitting on a chunk of clay against the wall, and explained how he and Becky had watched the flame flicker and die out.

The boys started to lower their voices to whispers now, as the silence and darkness of the place weighed heavily on their mood. They continued forward and soon entered and followed Tom's other passageway until they arrived at the "jumping-off place." The candles showed that it wasn't actually a cliff, but simply a steep clay slope about twenty or thirty feet tall. Tom whispered:

"Now I'll show you something, Huck."

He raised his candle high and said:

"Look as far around the corner as you can. Do you see that? There—on the big rock over there—made with candle smoke."

"Tom, it's a cross!"

"Now where's your Number Two? 'under the cross,' right? That's exactly where I saw Injun Joe stick up his candle, Huck!"

Huck gazed at the mysterious symbol for a moment, then spoke with a trembling voice:

"Tom, let's get out of here!"

"What! and leave the treasure?"

"Yes—leave it. Injun Joe's ghost is definitely lurking around there."

"No it isn't, Huck, no it isn't. It would haunt the place where he died—way out at the mouth of the cave—five miles from here."

"No, Tom, it wouldn't. It would stay near the money. I understand how ghosts behave, and you do too."

Tom started to worry that Huck might be right. Doubts began forming in his thoughts. But soon an idea came to him—

"Listen here, Huck, we're acting like complete fools! Injun Joe's ghost isn't going to show up anywhere near a cross!"

The point was well made. It had its impact.

"Tom, I hadn't thought of that. But you're right. That cross is lucky for us. I think we should climb down there and search for that box."

Tom went first, carving rough steps into the clay hillside as he made his way down. Huck followed behind him. Four passages branched off from the small cave where the massive rock was positioned. The boys explored three of these tunnels without finding anything. In the passage closest to the base of the rock, they discovered a small alcove with a makeshift bed of blankets laid out on the ground, along with an old suspender, some bacon rinds, and the well-chewed bones of two or three chickens. However, there was no money box to be found. The boys searched and searched this spot thoroughly, but their efforts were futile. Tom said:

"He said under the cross. Well, this comes closest to being under the cross. It can't be under the rock itself, because that sits solid on the ground."

They searched everywhere one more time, and then sat down feeling defeated. Huck couldn't think of anything to suggest. After a while, Tom said:

"Look here, Huck, there are footprints and some candle wax on the clay around one side of this rock, but not on the other sides. Now, what do you think that means? I bet the money is buried under the rock. I'm going to dig in the clay."

"That's not a bad idea, Tom!" said Huck excitedly.

Tom's "real Barlow" was out immediately, and he hadn't dug four inches before he hit wood.

"Hey, Huck! Do you hear that?"

Huck started digging and scratching at the ground. Soon they uncovered and pulled away several boards. The boards had been hiding a natural crack in the earth that went underneath the rock. Tom climbed down into this opening and stretched his candle as far under the rock as possible, but he said he couldn't see where the crack ended. He suggested they explore it. He bent down and crawled through; the narrow passage sloped downward little by little. He followed the twisting path, first turning right, then turning left, with Huck following close behind him. After a while, Tom rounded a sharp bend and called out:

"My goodness, Huck, look here!"

It was definitely the treasure chest, sitting in a cozy small cave alongside an empty gunpowder barrel, a few rifles in leather cases, two or three pairs of worn moccasins, a leather belt, and various other items thoroughly soaked from water dripping down.

"Finally found it!" Huck exclaimed, digging through the tarnished coins with his hand. "Wow, we're really rich now, Tom!"

"Huck, I always thought we'd find it. It's just too good to believe, but we definitely have it! Listen—let's not waste time here. Let's get it out of here. Let me see if I can lift the box."

It weighed approximately fifty pounds. Tom was able to lift it in a clumsy manner, but he couldn't carry it comfortably.

"I thought so," he said. "They carried it like it was heavy that day at the haunted house. I noticed that. I think I was right to consider bringing the little bags along."

The money was quickly placed in the bags and the boys carried it up to the cross rock.

"Now let's get the guns and other things," said Huck.

"No, Huck—leave them there. They're exactly what we need when we go robbing. We'll keep them there all the time, and we'll hold our secret meetings there, too. It's a perfect hidden spot for our gatherings."

"What orgies?"

"I don't know. But robbers always have orgies, and of course we've got to have them, too. Come on, Huck, we've been in here a long time. It's getting late, I think. I'm hungry, too. We'll eat and smoke when we get to the boat."

They soon came out into the cluster of sumac bushes, looked around carefully, saw that no one was there, and were quickly eating lunch and smoking in their small boat. As the sun began to set toward the horizon, they pushed off and started moving. Tom glided along the shoreline through the extended twilight, talking happily with Huck, and reached land shortly after darkness fell.

"Now, Huck," Tom said, "we'll hide the money in the loft of the widow's woodshed, and I'll come up in the morning and we'll count it and divide it up, and then we'll find a place out in the woods for it where it will be safe. Just stay quiet here and watch the stuff while I run and grab Benny Taylor's little wagon; I won't be gone a minute."

He vanished and soon came back with the wagon, placed the two small sacks inside it, tossed some old rags over them, and set off, pulling his load behind him. When the boys arrived at the Welshman's house, they paused to catch their breath. Just as they were getting ready to continue, the Welshman emerged and said:

"Hello, who's that?"

"Huck and Tom Sawyer."

"Great! Come with me, boys, you're making everyone wait. Here—hurry up, run ahead—I'll pull the wagon for you. Well, it's not as light as it could be. Do you have bricks in there?—or scrap metal?"

"Old metal," said Tom.

"I thought as much; the boys in this town will put in more effort and waste more time searching for seventy-five cents' worth of scrap metal to sell to the foundry than they would to earn twice that amount doing regular work. But that's human nature—hurry along, hurry along!"

The boys wanted to know what the rush was all about.

"Don't worry about it; you'll understand when we reach the Widow Douglas' house."

Huck spoke with a hint of worry—since he had grown accustomed to being wrongly blamed over the years:

"Mr. Jones, we haven't been doing nothing."

The Welshman laughed.

"Well, I don't know, Huck, my boy. I don't know about that. Aren't you and the widow good friends?"

"Yes. Well, she's been a good friend to me, anyway."

"All right, then. What do you want to be afraid for?"

This question hadn't been completely resolved in Huck's sluggish thoughts when he suddenly found himself being ushered, together with Tom, into Mrs. Douglas' living room. Mr. Jones parked the wagon close to the entrance and came in behind them.

The place was brilliantly lit, and everyone who mattered in the village was present. The Thatchers were there, the Harpers, the Rogerses, Aunt Polly, Sid, Mary, the minister, the newspaper editor, and many others, all wearing their finest clothes. The widow welcomed the boys as warmly as anyone could possibly welcome two such disheveled-looking creatures. They were covered in mud and candle wax. Aunt Polly turned bright red with embarrassment, and scowled while shaking her head at Tom. However, no one felt as uncomfortable as the two boys themselves. Mr. Jones said:

"Tom wasn't home yet, so I gave up on him; but I ran into him and Huck right at my door, so I just brought them along quickly."

"And you did exactly the right thing," said the widow. "Come with me, boys."

She brought them to a bedroom and said:

"Now go wash up and get dressed. Here are two brand-new outfits—shirts, socks, everything you need. They belong to Huck—no, don't thank him, Huck—Mr. Jones bought one set and I bought the other. But they'll fit both of you perfectly. Put them on. We'll wait down here—come back down once you're all cleaned up."

Then she left.

Chapter XXXIV

Huck said: "Tom, we can escape if we can find a rope. The window isn't high from the ground."

"Darn! Why do you want to run away?"

"Well, I'm not used to that kind of crowd. I can't stand it. I'm not going down there, Tom."

"Oh, darn! It's nothing at all. I don't mind it one bit. I'll take care of you."

Sid appeared.

"Tom," he said, "your aunt has been waiting for you all afternoon. Mary got your Sunday clothes ready, and everyone's been worrying about you. Tell me—isn't that grease and clay on your clothes?"

"Now, Mr. Siddy, you just mind your own business. What's all this commotion about, anyway?"

"It's one of the widow's parties that she's always throwing. This time it's for the Welshman and his sons, because of that trouble they helped her get out of the other night. And listen—I can tell you something, if you want to know."

"Well, what?"

"Well, old Mr. Jones is planning to surprise everyone here tonight, but I happened to overhear him telling my aunt about it today as if it were a secret. I suppose it's not much of a secret anymore though. Everyone knows about it—even the widow, despite how she pretends she doesn't. Mr. Jones was determined that Huck should be here—he couldn't pull off his big secret without Huck being present, you see!"

"What secret are you talking about, Sid?"

"About Huck following the robbers to the widow's house. I think Mr. Jones was planning to make a big deal out of his surprise, but I bet it's going to fall pretty flat."

Sid laughed quietly with deep contentment and satisfaction.

"Sid, was it you that told?"

"Oh, don't worry about who it was. Someone told me—that's all that matters."

"Sid, there's only one person in this town mean enough to do that, and that's you. If you had been in Huck's place you would have sneaked down the hill and never told anybody about the robbers. You can't do anything but mean things, and you can't stand to see anybody praised for doing good ones. There—no thanks, as the widow says"—and Tom boxed Sid's ears and helped him to the door with several kicks. "Now go and tell auntie if you dare—and tomorrow you'll catch it!"

A few minutes later, the widow's guests had gathered around the dinner table, while a dozen children sat at small side tables in the same room, following the custom of that region and era. When the appropriate moment arrived, Mr. Jones delivered his brief speech, expressing gratitude to the widow for the honor she was bestowing upon him and his sons, but he mentioned that there was another person whose humility—

And so on and so forth. He revealed his secret about Huck's role in the adventure with all the dramatic flair he could muster, but the surprise it created was mostly fake and not as loud and enthusiastic as it could have been under better circumstances. Still, the widow put on a pretty good show of amazement, and showered Huck with so many compliments and so much praise that he almost forgot how uncomfortable his new clothes felt in the face of the completely unbearable discomfort of being the center of everyone's attention and everyone's praise.

The widow explained that she intended to provide Huck with a home in her house and ensure he received an education; she also mentioned that when she had enough money available, she would help him start a small business. This was Tom's opportunity. He said:

"Huck doesn't need it. Huck's rich."

Nothing but the group's good manners held back the expected polite laughter at this amusing joke. But the silence felt somewhat uncomfortable. Tom interrupted it:

"Huck has money. You might not believe it, but he has plenty of it. Oh, you don't need to smile—I think I can prove it to you. Just wait a moment."

Tom ran outside. The group looked at each other with confused interest—and questioningly at Huck, who couldn't speak.

"Sid, what's wrong with Tom?" said Aunt Polly. "He—well, there's just no figuring that boy out. I never—"

Tom walked in, struggling under the weight of his heavy sacks, and Aunt Polly stopped speaking mid-sentence. Tom dumped the pile of gold coins onto the table and said:

"There—what did I tell you? Half of it's Huck's and half of it's mine!"

The sight left everyone completely speechless. Everyone stared, and no one said a word for several moments. Then everyone demanded an explanation all at once. Tom said he could provide one, and he proceeded to do so. The story was lengthy, but packed with fascinating details. There was hardly any interruption from anyone to disturb the captivating flow of his narrative. When he had finished, Mr. Jones said:

"I thought I had prepared a little surprise for this occasion, but it doesn't amount to anything now. This one makes it seem mighty small, I'm willing to admit."

The money was counted. The total came to just over twelve thousand dollars. It was more than anyone present had ever seen at one time before, although several people were there who owned property worth considerably more than that amount.

Chapter XXXV

The reader can be assured that Tom's and Huck's sudden fortune created an enormous commotion in the small, impoverished village of St. Petersburg. Such an enormous amount, all in real money, seemed almost unbelievable. People discussed it endlessly, obsessed over it, and celebrated it until many citizens' sanity began to crack under the pressure of this unhealthy frenzy. Every "haunted" house in St. Petersburg and the surrounding villages was torn apart, board by board, with foundations excavated and searched thoroughly for buried treasure—and this wasn't done by children, but by grown men—quite serious, practical men at that, some of them. Wherever Tom and Huck showed up, people sought their company, praised them, and gazed at them in wonder. The boys couldn't recall their words ever carrying any importance before; but now everything they said was valued and repeated; every action they took appeared somehow extraordinary; they had clearly lost their ability to do or say ordinary things; furthermore, their personal histories were examined and found to show signs of remarkable uniqueness. The local newspaper printed biographical articles about the boys.

The Widow Douglas invested Huck's money at six percent interest, and Judge Thatcher did the same with Tom's money at

Aunt Polly's request. Each boy now had an income that was absolutely enormous—a dollar for every weekday of the year and half the Sundays. This was exactly what the minister earned—no, it was what he was promised—he usually couldn't actually collect it. A dollar and twenty-five cents a week would pay for a boy's room, board, and schooling in those simple old days—and cover his clothing and laundry as well.

Judge Thatcher had developed a very high opinion of Tom. He said that no ordinary boy would have ever managed to get his daughter out of the cave. When Becky told her father, in complete confidence, how Tom had taken her punishment at school, the Judge was clearly moved; and when she asked for forgiveness for the enormous lie that Tom had told in order to transfer that punishment from her shoulders to his own, the Judge said with great emotion that it was a noble, generous, and magnanimous lie—a lie that deserved to hold its head high and march through history alongside George Washington's famous truth about the hatchet! Becky thought her father had never appeared so tall and magnificent as when he paced the floor and stamped his foot while saying that. She went immediately and told Tom about it.

Judge Thatcher hoped that Tom would become either a distinguished lawyer or a distinguished soldier someday. He explained that he planned to ensure Tom would be accepted into the National Military Academy and then receive training at the finest law school in the nation, so that Tom would be prepared for either profession or possibly both.

Huck Finn's wealth and the fact that he was now under the Widow Douglas' protection introduced him into society—no, dragged him into it, threw him into it—and his suffering was almost more than he could endure. The widow's servants kept him clean and tidy, his hair combed and brushed, and they put him to bed each night in unfriendly sheets that didn't have a single little spot or stain that he could hold close to his heart and recognize as a friend. He had to eat with a knife and fork; he had to use a napkin, cup, and plate; he had to study his lessons, he had to attend church; he had to speak so properly that talking became tasteless in his mouth; wherever he looked, the bars and chains of civilization surrounded him and tied him up completely.

He courageously endured his suffering for three weeks, and then one day he disappeared. For two full days the widow searched for him everywhere, filled with worry. The townspeople were deeply concerned; they looked everywhere, they even dragged the river searching for his body. Early on the third morning Tom Sawyer cleverly went searching among some old empty barrels behind the deserted slaughterhouse, and inside one of them he discovered the runaway. Huck had been sleeping there; he had just eaten breakfast consisting of some stolen scraps of food, and was now resting comfortably with his pipe. He was disheveled, his hair uncombed, and dressed in the same old tattered rags that had made him charming back when he was free and content. Tom woke him up, explained all the worry he had caused, and encouraged him to return home. Huck's face lost its peaceful satisfaction and became sad. He said:

"Don't talk about it, Tom. I've tried it, and it doesn't work; it doesn't work, Tom. It's not for me; I'm not used to it. The widow is good to me, and friendly; but I can't stand those ways. She makes me get up at the same time every morning; she makes me wash, they comb me until I'm completely disheveled; she won't let me sleep in the woodshed; I have to wear those awful clothes that just smother me, Tom; they don't seem to let any air get through them, somehow; and they're so perfectly nice that I can't sit down, or lie down, or roll around anywhere; I haven't slid on a cellar door for—well, it seems like years; I have to go to church and sweat and sweat—I hate those terrible sermons! I can't catch a fly in there, I can't chew. I have to wear shoes all Sunday. The widow eats by a bell; she goes to bed by a bell; she gets up by a bell—everything's so awfully regular a person can't stand it."

"Well, everybody does that way, Huck."

"Tom, it doesn't make any difference. I'm not like everybody else, and I can't stand it. It's awful to be tied up like this. And food comes too easy—I don't take any interest in meals that way. I have to ask to go fishing; I have to ask to go swimming—darn it if I don't have to ask to do everything. Well, I had to talk so nicely it wasn't any comfort—I had to go up in the attic and let loose for a while, every day, to get a taste in my mouth, or I would have died, Tom. The widow wouldn't let me smoke; she wouldn't let me yell, she wouldn't let me yawn, or stretch, or scratch, in front of people—" [Then with a spasm of special irritation and injury]—"And darn it, she prayed all the time! I never saw such a woman! I had to leave, Tom—I just had to. And besides, that school's going to open, and I would have had to go to it—well, I wouldn't stand that, Tom. Look here, Tom, being rich isn't what it's cracked up to be. It's just worry and worry, and sweat and sweat, and wishing you were dead all the time. Now these clothes suit me, and this barrel suits me, and I'm never going to give them up anymore. Tom, I never would have gotten into all this trouble if it hadn't been for that money; now you just take my share of it along with yours, and give me a dime sometimes—not many times, because I don't give a darn for a thing unless it's reasonably hard to get—and you go and make excuses for me with the widow."

"Oh, Huck, you know I can't do that. It isn't fair; and besides, if you'll try this thing just a little while longer, you'll come to like it."

"Like it! Yes—the way I'd like a hot stove if I had to sit on it long enough. No, Tom, I won't be rich, and I won't live in those cursed suffocating houses. I like the woods, and the river, and barrels, and I'll stick to them, too. Darn it all! just as we'd gotten guns, and a cave, and everything just set up to rob, here this darned foolishness has got to come up and spoil it all!"

Tom saw his opportunity—

"Listen here, Huck, being rich isn't going to stop me from becoming a robber."

"No! Oh, my goodness; are you being completely serious, Tom?"

"I'm being completely serious right now. But Huck, we can't let you join the gang if you're not respectable, you know."

Huck's happiness was crushed.

"Won't you let me in, Tom? Didn't you let me become a pirate?"

"Yes, but that's different. A robber has more class than a pirate does—generally speaking. In most countries they hold very high positions in the nobility—dukes and that sort of thing."

"Now, Tom, haven't you always been friendly to me? You wouldn't shut me out, would you, Tom? You wouldn't do that, now, would you, Tom?"

"Huck, I really don't want to do this, and I hate having to say it—but what would everyone think? They'd go around saying, 'Ha! Tom Sawyer's Gang! What a bunch of lowlifes!' They'd be talking about you, Huck. You wouldn't want that, and neither would I."

Huck remained quiet for a while, wrestling with his thoughts. At last he said:

"Well, I'll go back to the widow for a month and deal with it and see if I can learn to tolerate it, if you'll let me belong to the gang, Tom."

"All right, Huck, it's amazing! Come on, old friend, and I'll ask the widow to go easier on you a little, Huck."

"Will you, Tom—will you do it? That's great. If she eases up on some of the harshest rules, I'll smoke in secret and swear in private, and I'll push through this or die trying. When are you going to start the gang and become robbers?"

"Oh, right away. We'll gather the boys and maybe hold the initiation tonight."

"Have the what?"

"Have the initiation."

"What's that?"

"It means promising to support each other, and never reveal the gang's secrets, even if you're torn to pieces, and to kill anyone and their entire family who harms a member of the gang."

"That's wonderful—that's really wonderful, Tom, I tell you."

"Well, I'm sure it is. And all that swearing has to be done at midnight, in the loneliest, most awful place you can find—a haunted house is the best, but they're all torn down now."

"Well, midnight's good, anyway, Tom."

"Yes, that's right. And you have to swear on a coffin, and sign it with blood."

"Now, that's more like it! Why, it's a million times better than pirating. I'll stick with the widow until I die, Tom; and if I become a really great robber, and everybody's talking about it, I think she'll be proud that she took me in from the cold."

CONCLUSION

So this chronicle comes to an end. Since it is strictly the history of a boy, it must stop here; the story could not continue much further without becoming the history of a man. When someone writes a novel about adults, they know exactly where to stop—that is, with a marriage; but when they write about young people, they must stop wherever they can do so most appropriately.

Most of the people who appear in this book are still alive and doing well. Someday it might be worthwhile to continue the story of the younger characters and see what kind of adults they became; therefore it would be best not to reveal any details about that part of their lives right now.

Thank You For Reading

You've Just Read a Piece of the Greatest Library Ever Rebuilt

Thank you for reading.

This book is one of thousands we're restoring, reimagining, and translating as part of the **Modern Library of Alexandria** — a global movement to preserve and share humanity's most important ideas.

What was once lost to fire and time is now rising again — not just as memory, but as living, breathing knowledge, freely accessible to all.

What You Can Do Next:

- **Keep Reading.**

  Discover more legendary works — in beautiful print, audiobook, or digital form — at LibraryofAlexandria.com.

- **Build Your Own Library.**

  Every title is available as a paperback, hardcover, or collectible boxset — at true printing cost. Craft a personal library worthy of display.

- **Spread the Light.**

  Share this book. Tell others about the movement. Help us translate every timeless work into every language, so no reader is ever left behind.

By finishing this book, you've already taken part in something extraordinary.

Join us at LibraryofAlexandria.com

Together, we're rebuilding the greatest library the world has ever known.

With appreciation,

The Modern Library of Alexandria Team

Visit:
www.libraryofalexandria.com
Or scan the code below:

www.ingramcontent.com/pod-product-compliance
Lightning Source LLC
Chambersburg PA
CBHW011405010726
47495CB00009B/2788

* 9 7 8 1 8 0 6 2 9 8 8 9 1 *